From the Beginning to the Very End

The Solution to the Drug Problem in the United States

Arthur H. Misener

authorHOUSE®

AuthorHouse™
1663 Liberty Drive, Suite 200
Bloomington, IN 47403
www.authorhouse.com
Phone: 1-800-839-8640

First published by AuthorHouse 2/14/2008

ISBN: 978-1-4343-3528-9 (e)
ISBN: 978-1-4343-3527-2 (sc)

Library of Congress Control Number: 2007906423

Printed in the United States of America
Bloomington, Indiana

This book is printed on acid-free paper.

Dedicated to Andrew Manzardo & Janet Gabrielson without their long hours of assistance this book could not have been pubished. Thank You !

CHARACTERS

Pregnant Mexican Mother	Marie Lopez
Child and Congressman	Caesar Markos
Caesar's Parents	Patricia & Juan Markos
Caesar's best Friend	Leo Borrow
Village Boss	Hittose Vicea
Captain	Adam Collins
Admiral	Dale Owings
Commander & His Wife	Bill Story & Willa Story
Story' Daughter	Lura & Her School Fair Haven
Bill Story's Co-Pilot	Stanley Moore
Story's Plane Captain	Haver Washington
Story's Plane Loader	Cliff Hill
Story's Second Loader	Toby Marshall
Navigator	James Waltham
Ship # 1	Pagan Island
Ship's Second Name	Alan Chime
President	Hale Mclour His wife Merna
President's son	Richard-His school—Fort Lee
White House Security Chief	Maxwell Chase
Other security People	Norm Patterson, Vera Simms, Charles Pitt

Provost Marshall	Bill Manning
Camera Operator	Pete Malcolm
	Petty Officer First Class
San Diego Naval Shipyard	Commander Bill Wilson
Gulf Port Shipyard	Cal Williams
Waitress	Dixie North
	—Restaurant Moving On
San Diego Port Captain	Pete Marcona
Fertilizer Plant owners	Cody & Glen Jacobs
Rice Destination	World Hunger—
	St. Louis Mo.
Entomologist	James Q. Adams
Jax Police Chief	Vernon Porter
Jax Air Station Head	Commander Joe Anton
Jax Executive Officer	Lt. Commander Harry Carter
	& Wife Peggy & daughter Megan

Board of Directors

Customs	George Beck
AFT	Henry Green
Coast Guard	Hale Laden
Border Patrol	Mark Kent
Naval Intell	Roger Ralston
Marines Major	Brad Wilson
Army Major	Will Milford
NSA	Louis Newman
California St Police Captain	Woody Miner,
Naval Intell-pilot	Lt. Commander
	Sara West-Helen Abel

THE BEGINNING

Rain was coming down in sheets in a little crossroad town just south of Tijuana, Mexico where Maria Lopez was packing everything she owned for her trip to San Diego California. She wrapped herself in all the clothes she had and covered herself in a plastic sheet she brought from the little dispensary where she worked for the last seven months.

She was to meet the bus at five a.m. up at next corner. When she got there, she met eleven others. The old bus finally came out of the heavy rain to where they all waited. The old bus did not look like it would make it to the border let alone to San Diego where Maria was going to have her baby. They all crowded on the bus, happy to be out of the rain.

Most of the people rode the bus every day north to work in rich people's homes. They sat up in the front as if they had assigned seats. Maria sat in the rear with three others that did not have the necessary green cards that got them past the man at the border that checked them through.

Next the driver came back to collect the balance of the money the people owed for being smuggled north to United States. Maria gave him the balance of the five hundred dollars she owed. A little old woman who sat next to Maria paid her money to the driver and introduced herself to Maria as Anna. She was going to San Diego to help her daughter who was going through a very difficult pregnancy. This was to be her first grandchild and she was so excited she could hardly wait.

The old bus bounded along for almost an hour, not very fast because of the heavy rain, and finally coming to a stop just short of the border guards' shack. A guard was inside the shack out of the rain that was coming down harder. After few minutes they could hear loud voices between the driver and the officer. The driver got back on the bus, went to the rear where Maria sat and said the man he normally does business with was transferred to the day shift and this new man wanted twenty-five dollars more from each of the four persons that had no green cards. He said they had to pay the extra money now or get off the bus right here and no money paid would be returned. Anna started to cry and said she had no more money and if she were put off the bus here she would never get to see her first grandchild born. She said it would be impossible to save enough to make the trip again. Maria reached into her bra and paid the driver for Anna. There was no way she could see Anna put off the bus after all they had gone through to get to this point.

When they finally reached San Diego, the bus let Maria off two blocks from the hospital where she wanted to have her baby. She covered herself with all her clothes and the plastic and headed for the hospital admittance desk. It was still early and the only person there was an old woman reading her newspaper. When Maria told her she was here to have her baby the woman, with out looking up, handed her a clipboard and said to fill it out in English if she could. This was no problem for Maria as she had taken English as a major in collage. After returning the filled out papers to the old woman she and was told that it would cost her two hundred dollars. Maria took out the remaining money from her bra and found she was twenty-five dollars short. Maria said that she thought it would be less money and that she only had one hundred and seventy five dollars. The money she gave to Anna on the bus caused her to be short the necessary amount she needed.

The old woman looked down her nose and said that all the Mexican women come here with no money and expect the doctors to deliver their babies for free. She advised Maria to get a midwife as they were much cheaper. Maria said that as a nurse she had seen the work of some of them and wanted no part of it.

Maria sat back down and started to cry. She was cold and wet and the fact she was about ready to deliver did not help matters at all. When she felt a warm hand touch hers, she looked up to see a smiling face. The smiling face introduced herself as Pat Markos and said "Things cannot be so bad that they cannot be worked out. Let us talk about it and see if we can brighten things up a bit."

After she wiped her eyes and stopped crying, Maria started to tell Pat her story. Maria said that she was the first in the family to finish college having graduated from nursing school after a long four years. Her mother threw a big party that all her friends and the whole clan attended. There was plenty of food and lots to drink. She had a few drinks and not being used to it, she started to feel the effects of it early. Maria said that she went up to her room, lay across the bed, and before long she was in a deep sleep. "I do not know how long I was asleep when I felt someone on the bed with me. It was a man who lifted up my dress and pulled down my panties. He entered me before I was fully awake, it did not take long. When he got down off the bed and wiped himself on the bed covers, I recognized him. It was my mother's younger brother Mickeal.

I was afraid to tell anyone for if my brothers found out they would slit his throat. It was difficult not telling anyone even when I was having morning sickness. Before long my stomach was starting to swell. I moved away, telling my mother, that now I was a nurse I wanted to work in a small village serving the poor. I moved to a small village just south of Tijuana. No one back home knew I was pregnant and I wrote telling them I was doing real well. After seven months working in the dispensary, I saved up enough money to come to California to have my baby."

Maria told Pat about giving money to Anna that left her short of having enough money to pay for a doctor to deliver her child. She just could not sit there and have Anna put off the bus when the old woman had saved the money to see her first grandchild born.

Pat asked her if she was going to take the baby back to Mexico once it was born. Maria said "Oh god no, if my mother found out, her brother would fear for his life. I will leave the baby here for someone to adopt and go back as if nothing happened."

Pat told Maria that it did not look like she would deliver her baby today and suggested they go back to her place and have something to eat. On the way home in Pat's old pickup truck, Pat told Maria that she was at the hospital that morning because her husband fell at work and injured his back. After some hot food, Maria lay down on the bed and went fast asleep.

When she woke up Pat announced that she had a solution to Maria's problem. She asked if she would rather leave her baby with someone she knew than with a stranger. Pat then told Maria that she and her husband had tried to have a child for years with no success. Here is my plan, "When you go back to the hospital, fill my name in place of yours and my husband as the father... I will pay your hospital bill in full and give you enough money to go back to your family. It is a win, win plan as we will get a baby and you can go back to start your life all over. We own a store that earns enough money in order to raise your baby in a manner you would have liked to do."

The next morning Maria delivered a beautiful baby boy. Pat went up to her husband's room and told him of her plan; he looked surprised and asked her if she could get away with it? Pat said "We will know in a few days." On the way home, they picked up all the things a new baby would need and while Maria was nursing the baby, Pat went down to the bureau of vital statistics and applied for a birth certificate for the baby. She picked Juan up from the hospital and on the way back home stopped off and picked up the birth certificate that the clerk said would be ready.

"What did you name the baby?" Pat answered saying that when she was in school she remembered reading about Julius Caesar so she named him Caesar Juan Markos. "Do you like it?" Maria replied she thought it was a strong and beautiful name and felt sure that the baby boy would live up to it.

After two weeks of nursing the baby to give him a good start Pat drove Maria to the border and handed her an envelope containing five hundred dollars. Pat kissed her and said you may feel free to visit any time as Aunt Maria. They kissed again, turned their backs, and never saw each other again.

When Caesar was only two, he had the run of the store and with his little broom would sweep up the place. He was a smart child and at the age of three, Juan was teaching him numbers. Juan taught him to write his name as well as his mother's and father's. Juan was not able to return to work because of his back injury and received a small worker's compensation check each month. He read to Caesar, everything from children's books to things out of the newspapers, all day long and before bedtime. He read only in English for he reasoned that was the language of business and you had to be good at it if you wished to succeed. His goal was to have a son that would rise in the business world. Juan taught Caesar numbers and how to use the cash register.

When Caesar went to school he was always dressed in a white shirt and blue tie so it did not take long before the kids all called him "Tie," which was not bad - better then what some kids were called. The white shirt and tie were not a good dress for playing sports so he kept older clothes over at his best friend Leo Borrow's house. One day his mother was out for a walk and decided to stop off and walk home with her son. Soon she did not believe what she saw as here was Caesar in old clothes playing ball. The next day he was back in white shirt and blue tie.

Caesar was a brilliant young boy and far above the rest of his class because of his training at home. He excelled in mathematics and could read three grades ahead of the rest of the class. Because he could speak both Spanish and English, he would stay after school to tutor the more backward children.

One day a nicely dressed man came in the store to talk to his parents and he could speak fluently in several languages. This man greatly impressed Caesar; he dressed well and had an air of importance. His name was Hittose Vicea and he always made a point to spend some time talking to Caesar. Caesar could carry on conversations with adults with no trouble at all.

Hittose called a meeting at the old shoe factory that was being converted into a home for the poor and aged and he wanted Pat to act as mistress of ceremonies. Pat was well known and liked because of giving food to those who had nothing. Pat took the stand and introduced Hittose who was a member of the city council that represented their neighborhood. Hittose started out by saying that the area where they lived would be known as the 'village' and not the 'barrio' because 'barrio' means a poor run-down area.

Hittose then said "We will collect money according to your income, and just like taxes if you have little, you pay nothing. The money will be used only in our village to hire security and fix up some of the vacant houses. These houses will be rented out and the rent money will go into the pot to help fix up more houses. Let me see hands of people who are afraid to go out of their homes after dark."

Many hands went up - and not only those of women. "Okay", he said, "that will all change right away. We will block off all streets at night except the main road. I see that all of this is far above your heads right now so let me say this, if in six months this plan does not work out I will give you back all the money you have paid in. That is how sure I am that this will work. Fair enough? Hittose continued "We will teach English to adults as well as children and if you learn it you will get better jobs and make more money." One man got up and said out loud "Yeah, and pay more into your tax plan." Hittose said, "That is right, but you get to keep eighty per cent of your income."

Security people were brought in and after a few knocks on heads and a black eye or two the security system was starting to work. Those who decided not to behave were kicked out of the village and not allowed back in. A bank was set up so people did not have their money at home for someone to borrow and probably not pay back. The bank would lend money at a fair rate and balances would be posted monthly.

By having their own security force, the city did not have to send in city police unless Vicea called for them. This made the commissioner happy and qualified the village for a subsidy from the city and the state. This helped to build up the treasury to spend money to fix up more run-down houses. Those were then rented out and brought in more money. Here was a system that fed on itself. The city was happy to support any request from Hittose Vicea so the grant money would come pouring in...

Crime was down to domestic problems that were generally solved by representatives of the family relations committee who stopped around and saw the people involved. This worked out when they were told that we all had to work together. Identification cards were given out to members of the village so that if they were picked up in town by police on minor offences they were brought back to the village where security would handle the situation.

Villagers were learning English and are finding their income going up. The idea of the village was spreading to other Spanish speaking communities and Hittose Vicea's picture was in the local papers all the time.

Caesar will never forget the time when walking home from school the fire engine came down his street to a fire that completely consumed his mother's house and store. The only way out was the inside stairs that ran from the second floor down through the store. Pat had gone up to help Juan down, but because off his back injuries he had difficulty with steps, and as a result they both perished. While standing there feeling so helpless he felt a hand on his shoulder, it was Hittose, the man he had admired for years. He took Caesar to Leo's house and asked Mrs. Borrow if she would take care of Caesar for a while and that he would pay all expenses plus extra to help Caesar through these hard times. She said sure, as he is here all the time, more then he is at home any way.

After high school, Hittose used his influence to get Caesar into college and law school where he graduated from both with honors. He helped pay all expenses with the understanding the Caesar would serve the village for at least three-years. Hittose set him up with an office just outside of the village, that way he could serve clients from both outside interests and those of the village people too.

Word got back to Hittose that Caesar was mixed up in the drug business. Hittose called Caesar to his office and after they were seated, asked him directly. Caesar admitted that there might be some truth in that. Hittose said" That is a very dangerous business. Do you remember those two men that burned alive in their car on the south side just after your parents' fire? They were the men that torched your parents' store because they would not sell drugs for them. You see there were four persons that died because of drugs. Be very careful and promise me one thing that you will never involve the village or its people in any of your drug business." Caesar reached out his hand, shook hands with Hittose, and promised what Hittose asked.

A few weeks went by and Caesar showed up at Vicea's office, after some small talk. Caesar asked a favor. He said that he had to meet somebody down on the docks tonight and would Hittose come along to watch his back. Because of his relationship with Caesar's parents, he agreed. He got a pistol that he had a license to carry from his desk. After dark, he rode with Caesar down to the docks where two men were already waiting. Hittose stayed back at the car and kept an eye on them. A loud argument broke out followed by gunshots. Caesar ran back to his car and said "Let's get the hell out of here!"

When the police investigated the deaths, they found two men dead with two guns that had not been fired.

Newspapers ran the story for a few days but dropped it in favor of a headline that said one of the men that was shot was a man running for re-election for the U.S. congress and now who will run in his place?

A meeting was held in a hall in the district that included the village to figure out who should be a candidate in the upcoming election. Caesar was the likely person and with Hittose backing him, he had no trouble getting elected. After the election, Hittose found out that Caesar was using boys from the village to push drugs in the city. He confronted Caesar and said we had an agreement, shook hands on it, and if your word is no good you will pay dearly for it some day. You will be very sorry.

It was one of southern California's beautiful mornings when a large car pulled up in the front of the Southern California Real Estate Company's office. Out stepped out a tall thin man in a dark tailored blue suit and after surveying the sign out front he let himself inside. Behind the desk was a young girl who asked if she could be of any help? He said he would like to see Mr. Bill Story. She said it was the first door on the right and Bill was buzzed. He got up to greet the man who asked for him and when he opened his door there stood an old friend of many years. "You old sea dog I have not seen you for some time. This cannot be navy business since you are in civvies and I have been out for three months now.

Let me introduce you to my daughter who is working the reception desk while our regular girl is on vacation. Laura, do you remember this man?" She looked at him long and hard, let out a scream, and said "Oh my god, its uncle Adam." Adam Collins hugged her and said "I am your godfather too. My, but you have grown since I saw you last."

The two went back into Bill's office where Bill asked if this was a business or social call. "It cannot be business for I retired three months ago." Adam said, "I wanted to be here for your retirement but I was in the Far East; how about you and Willa having dinner with me tonight?" Bill said I think you are up to something. I have served with you for so long and have seen that look in your eye to know that look. What is it Adam, I know it must be something concerning the navy." Adam said, "I will tell you and Willa this evening. You are still living in the same place. Yes? Fine I will see you both at seven." Bill said "If you have a few minutes, Willa should be right back." Adam replied that he had some stops to make and was sort of in a rush but would see them at seven.

At exactly seven the doorbell rang, Willa answered the door and Adam stepped in" Willa, you look the same as the day you got married, twenty years ago. You are something to look at with that black dress set off with those pearls." Willa gave Adam a big hug and said" You navy men are all alike when you see an attractive woman. You act as you have just gotten off the ship after a six month tour."

"We were sad to hear that Nancy passed away." Adam said then that they were married for forty years and all were good ones. Adam said, "I hope you picked out a nice expensive restaurant for I am hungry."

At the restaurant Adam looked at Bill and Willa and said, "I need Bill's help on a real big job the navy gave me. Help me on a covert operation as my executive officer. This takes in some flying duties Willa, and Bill is one of the best pilots I have ever seen. It will take six weeks to two months at the most."

Willa said, "Bill is getting antsy around the office and all the women he shows houses to want to take him home with them. It seems to let him fly off with you is the safest thing to do. I know that you do not have to ask him, hell, he would leave this minute. Okay, you can have him for two months, any longer I will come looking for you both with dogs." "Adam, promise you will bring him back safe."

Willa made reservations at the El Coronado Hotel for two nights and it did not long before she realized they were in the glide path of the North Island Naval Base landing strip. Every time a jet passed over them Bill would almost sit up in bed, it was as if he were up there with them. They swam during the day, danced at night, and made love the rest of the time.

Bill looked at the clothing list Adam gave him; mostly suntans and to his surprise some old uniforms. Adam picked Bill up before eight and drove out to

North Island where they met about thirty others already there. Everything was ready to go except a plane. Just then there was a roar and out of the sky came a twin-engine World War II C-47. They asked if these things still flew; God, I am younger then that plane, one said. Adam said, "Without that plane World War II would have lasted another six months as they carried supplies as well paratroopers."

Adam said, "Okay, let's get aboard and see if this plane will fly. They were in the air not much more than an hour when they circled over what looked like a huge junkyard, but instead of old cars the land was full of old planes. "This, gentleman is Arizona, the largest litter box in the country where you store anything made of metal and because it is so dry these planes are preserved forever." said Adam.

The plane made a smooth landing, not what these jet pilots were used to. They got out and looked around at two old hangers, one with quarters in the rear, just a few bunks and a couple of tables. Bill looked around for the air-conditioning and found they did not have any. Wow, in the middle of the desert and no air. He unpacked and strolled out to the hangers where a rag-tag group dressed in tee shirts, cut offs, or shorts was gathered. Adam said, "These planes go back to 1937 and they were no doubt one of the best planes ever built." Bill said, "I am a little curious what they have to do with us." Adam said, "You will all find out tomorrow, but first I want you to meet your co-pilot. Bill, I want you to meet Stanley Moore. Stanley, Bill Story here is one of the best pilots I ever flew with." After they left Stanley, Bill remarked, "My god, he is the age of my daughter." Adam said, 'Do not let looks fool you, these young ones are dammed good flyers. The man that is running the show there is your plane captain Haver Washington, the tall black man with muscles all men want and in all the right places. Right now, they are installing new engines in these old planes."

That evening they made up their crews - a pilot, co-pilot and a plane captain. An additional man will be added later. Bill felt good with a young co-pilot and a big strong man for a plane captain. The next morning Adam called his men together and said, "These planes came off the drawing boards in 1937 and after many modifications were put into service in 1939. We have modified the planes even more; we made the wings longer and two feet wider. In addition, we added new Pratt & Whitney 2800 engines in place of the old 1600s that were used up to this point - that's 2400 more horses. With the wider, longer wings, we added much larger flaps; our load now will be 10,000 pounds instead of 6600 maximum before. We will test the planes Wednesday starting with 6,000 pounds and increase the load each day until we get it up to the 10.000 mark necessary to complete our mission. Oh yes, the decks in the planes are equipped with rollers that raise and lower hydraulically making it easier to load. The first set allows cargo to be rolled in and the second set will rise to help push the loads to the rear and forward. One man pushes a hell of a load on these guys. Oh, one other thing you may have noticed on these larger engines is there are four wider blades on the propellers as this will give us the thrust we will need. Bill Story will take the first flight to see how they work out."

After chow, Bill sat with Haver Washington shooting the breeze and asked him how he became a first class petty officer at such a young age. "Well, Mister Story, I grew up in my uncle's garage. Starting at six and by the time I was twelve I could tune-up an engine better than any one in the garage. After I joined the navy, the word got around in officers' country that I could make their cars run faster and with more power then they ever thought possible. The higher officers had priority over my time and I was advanced even when there were no openings. After time I learned how to work the system, and here I am. I have been in the navy a year and a half. I love cars but I wanted to see how it was to work on planes. They are pretty much the same except if a car's engine stops the car just sits there - in the case of a plane, the plane starts to fall. Bill told Washington that Captain Collins was a great man and if he says it will fly, it will fly.

Bill Story took off the next morning and got the surprise of his life. This plane is different than anything he ever flew. It was a great big glider with powerful engines. The least movement of the controls and the plane responded beautifully. He let Stanley, his co-pilot take the controls to get the feel of this completely different type of plane. When they got back, they started taking off and landing with light loads.

The next morning they started with heavier loads. Stanley would look out the right window and call out the distance markers to see how far they had to go before the wheels left the ground. At first, they were way off their mark so they had to try a different approach. Washington suggested that they start with the brakes on and rev up the engines to near full throttle, then release the brakes. By George, remarked Story when he found out this would meet the distance requirements. With some instruction, the rest of the pilots soon found they could meet the standards for taking off but could not land in the required distance. Again, they had to work this problem out. Adam suggested the pilot control the plane while the co-pilot works the throttle and the pitch of the propellers as soon as they land. If before they cut back on the power they put the propellers in reverse they could slow the plane down. This gets tricky, if you reverse one engine more then the other the plane would spin like a top. One pilot hit his brakes too hard and set his plane up on its nose. After that, they trained much harder and it was not long before they had the drill down pat. Now they had to practice loading and unloading and for this, they added a fourth man to the crew of each plane. Bill Story got a petty officer third class, named Cliff Hill. He was a young blond man who took a lot of kidding because of his name but he took it with a smile.

All the training was over and at a meeting Captain Collins told them that they would take off for the first leg of their flight tomorrow. He wanted his men to write a letter home that will not be mailed unless you do not return. The letters will be given back to you when you come back. Get some sleep; we take off at 0800.

The sun was up and the crews were ready for the flight to Alameda, California, where their planes will be fitted with large plastic internal fuel tanks to carry them over long distances over water. While the workmen were installing these tanks, the crews were given a nice surprise. They were loaded into two large navy vans and given a tour of San Francisco. They went to Alcatraz and enjoyed locking each other in solitary confinement. All the men wore suntans with no insignias; this made the enlisted men more conformable. They ate in the best restaurants and took in some girly shows where the older men kidded the younger ones.

Back on the base, they checked the new tanks for leaks as a leak in the middle of the Pacific could be disastrous. On a long flight to Honolulu, they rotated seats to give all the crew a feel of the controls and a look of the instruments. Bill Story had said that you never know when they may have to help fly you back sometime. As they circled Pearl Harbor they all looked out and saw just about what the Japanese saw on that December morning back in 1941. No time for a tour this time; they take off at 0200. Bill picked up an additional crewmember; his name was Lt. James Walthem, a navigator. The next stop was Wake Island for refueling, a small speck on a map you had better not miss or you are in deep trouble.

On Wake, they only had time to refuel get a few hours sleep before their longest leg of the trip. As Cliff Hill was opening the large cargo door a gust of wind caught it and slammed it on his arm. Story and Washington examined it they decided that he had better have it looked at in the navy hospital. Sure enough, it was broken. Bill radioed Captain Collins who said he would pick up a replacement and meet up with them later.

Captain Collins met the incoming flight from Wake at an old World War II air base just south of Mindanao in the Philippines. Since Collins was flying in a jet, he could move around much faster. He had Hill's replacement with him. His name was Toby Marshall, an older second-class petty officer. Washington took Story aside and said "That man is black like me, but he does not look too smart or too honest so let's keep an eye on him." Story learned to take advice from Washington for he was smart and could read people. Captain ordered the planes to be fueled up and loaded with provisions and to meet with the security group, a mercenary platoon that is paid very well to provide their services. A man named Bill Manning, who said his title was provost marshal and carried the rank of major, headed them. His job was to guard the planes after they landed wherever the operation took them.

The next stop was a small island in the Gulf of Thailand called Zamboaga. What that means or why no one knows or for that matter cares. They took off at 0400 the next morning with the sun to their backs all the way. Before nightfall and with aid of Lt. James Walthem as navigator, they circled this small island. Looking down was this little speck in the Bay of Thailand. There was a good sized runway and large buildings but what surprised them was a large ship tied up on one side of the island where they were to unload their supplies.

The buildings were in good shape for they were not very old since they had been used in the Viet Nam war. The men ate and hit the sack. Manning posted his men outside to protect them from whatever there was out there. The next morning they had a great breakfast. Collins had brought a complete galley with him. Nothing makes a crew happier than good food. Later that morning the plastic internal gas tanks were removed and piled up over near the ship.

Captain Collins addressed the men and told them to get out of their clothes and put them in a sea bag. Next to each of them were new clothes right from the skin out. Over the new underwear was a set of blue coveralls. "Make sure the shoes fit as we do not want any sore feet in case you have to walk back. You may notice the name on the coveralls that shows you now work for Pacific Air. In a small bag next to the sea bags, you will put all personal items, your wallet any rings, metals of any sort including crosses or Star of David. We do not want anything to identify you with the United States. You do not know who you may run into on this mission and they may not like what you are carrying. You are issued a wristwatch and if you look at the back, there is a small compass. If you are downed, head due south, that is where we will look for you. In a small cotton bag, there is paper money and coins from this area. Three of the coins are gold. They are to be used to bribe anyone that may help you to the coast. The money is to be given back if you do not need it. We have plastic dog tags; wear them as you did your military ones. The numbers on your tags are the same as on your sea bags and personal effects bag. The planes are being stripped of U.S. markings and replaced with decals of Pacific Air. Pilots will wear green tags, air crew blue, and ground crew will have red. We have a record of your number; every thing will be locked up here for when you get back. All air crews will meet after dinner for further instructions."

"We will take off at 0900; the fog should be burned off over the jungle by then as we will be looking for a small landing strip cared out of the jungle. After take off, record your heading, and on return your heading will read 180 degrees from that. Lt. Waltham and Bill Manning with his security force will fly with Story. The people on the ground will set off yellow smoke signals. If we see no smoke, head on back here to this base we named K. The jungle base is named B. When you land go all the way to the end of the strip and make a 180 degree turn to your left that will put you into position to take off. Unload and get out as soon as you can. Last plane in is first plane out. Don't wait for the others; as soon as you are loaded take off. I did not mention that you would be bringing cargo out. What it contains is none of your business and, remember, this operation is top secret. Any talk even amongst your selves is forbidden and is punishable by court martial. Watch the men with the red flags on return and follow them to the unloading zone. After breakfast, warm up your planes; they are already loaded and ready to take off at 0900."

Bill Story took off with the others following. Waltham looked down and said, "Hell, there are no land marks, just green jungle." He followed his compass settings and sure enough, there was yellow smoke ahead. They landed as they practiced with the pilot at the controls and the co-pilot on the throttles and reverse on the propellers. Bill Manning's men got out and secured the perimeter. He told everyone not to go into the jungle because people go in and never come back out. The natives unloaded and loaded with the help of the aircrew. The pilots went over to a little shack to get a drink and one said "Where did they get lift trucks in the middle of the jungle?" One of the other pilots remarked, "Next time in why don't you ask them?"

When they returned, Story got in line to be unloaded and left the taxiing to Washington who had training to do so. He went over to meet Captain Collins who was anxious to hear how everything went. Bill said, "It went just as we practiced. Jim Waltham is all they say; he hit it right on he nose. I would like to have him with me one more time if I can." Collins said "Sure, there is nothing for him to do around here." Story and Collins went over and looked at the ship that was loading and unloading. Bill said, "This is an unusual ship. The wheelhouse leans forward like the Swedish ships and it has cranes forward and mid-ship."

The next day went just like the first and Bill had Waltham with him to help spot the landing strip. Bill told him "I will be glad to get out of here. This place gives me the creeps."

The other pilots were kidding Story saying that he used up the whole field to land. Story said "Yesterday

I was hauling men; today I was carrying cargo. Stanley saved my butt and when we get back to civilization, I will buy him the biggest steak I can find as he pulled my irons out of the fire."

The next two days were like the first and things went smoothly. Bill still had the navigator with him and it was good to have an extra set of eyes trying to find the needle in a haystack. After they got back showered and ate, Captain Collins called them all together and said, "We all want to get out of here and since there is just enough to make two light trips we will make two trips tomorrow."

The first load the next day was easy and it didn't take as long to load and unload. After lunch they went back for the last time. Bill knew the way in and out so he left the navigator back at base K. Things went bad. The lift trucks broke down and with the help of the air crews the slow process started. Bill Manning came over to Bill and asked if he had a crew member named Washington. Bill said "Yes, he is my plane captain and right now he is helping to unload the planes. Why do you need him?" Manning said, "I have to take him in to custody; he is wanted in the states for murder." Bill said, "How did you find that way out here in the jungle?" Manning said, "Never you mind, I have to lock him up until we leave." Story asked him, "Where is he going to from here; we do not even know where we are." Manning said, I am the provost marshal and what I say goes." Manning took Washington and locked him up in a little tin shack. Story sat on a log outside the shack and asked Washington, "What is this all about?"

Washington said that one night when he was to meet his wife to walk her home this drunk started to hit on her. When I got there we had words and he took a poke at me. I hit him back and he fell against a stone wall and didn't move. My wife said, "Oh, my god you've killed him." "We ran home and for a week watched the papers for some news. I was frightened for I was on probation for another fight when this big person started picking on some small kids. I work days and my wife works evenings so I do not see much of her. When I got off work one day instead of going to the gym like I always do, I was tired so I went home to take a shower. We share the upstairs bathroom with my mother-in-law. She has a powder room on the first floor but showers upstairs.

This day I hear the bathroom door open as I was drying off. I look up and my mother-in-law was standing there looking me over. She said I wanted to see what my daughter was getting in bed. I yelled, "Get out you crazy woman!" She said, "I know you are on probation and if I holler rape, you go to jail for five years. How do like that sonny?" We were having sex three or four times a week and my wife did not know about it. One day as I was finishing, this old woman said she wanted me to service her sister who lived next door. I knew that she had two more sisters down the street and figured she would call them all to get into the action."

"The next day I went down to the navy recruiter and told him I would sign up if he could take me right away. I told my wife I was going and that I would send her an allotment plus any money I made tuning cars. I sent her all that I had, but she wrote that I have to send more. Now comes the good part. She said that if I did not send more money, she would turn me in for killing the man that night. A friend of mine that works in my uncle's garage wrote me and told me he saw my wife the other day and she is eight months pregnant. Now, I have not been home for over a year, so there is no way that she is carrying my child."

Just then there was gunfire and not just rifle shots, more like machine guns and mortars. Bill Manning ran by and said the rollers were not operating on plane four so he and his men were leaving on it. Bill said, "What are you going to do about Washington?" Manning shouted back, "If you care about the black man get him out yourself." He then threw the keys on the ground. Story picked up the keys and tried to find the right one and gave up. He told Washington to stand back, took out his 45 automatic, and shot the lock off the door. Story and Washington were running to the plane when they saw Stanley get shot. Bill told Washington to warm the plane up and he would carry Stanley who didn't go over a hundred and forty pounds. Bill laid Stanley down gently even though he was dead. Bill got in the cockpit and was waiting for plane number two to get moving. Just then there were mortar shells falling all around them. One landed under the plane in front of them. Bill thought if that plane didn't move, neither could he. Finally, plane number two started to move just as a mortar shell went off underneath it.

As Bill was moving to take off, mortar shells were falling all around the planes. He said to himself, "God, I hope it did not do any damage to it. If plane number two does not move my plane cannot take off either." Plane two finally got in the air. Just then, his plane took quite a jolt as a mortar went off on his port side. He called to Washington and asked him to come forward and see if he could see any damage. Just then, a mortar shell came down through the overhead and went off inside the plane. Washington came forward, his face full of blood. After he cleared the trees and as Story was getting the first aid kit out he noticed part of Washington's nose was missing. He bandaged him up the best he could and asked about Marshall. Haver said his head was almost gone. "If it had gone off a second earlier the whole plane would have gone up. If I had not come forward to examine the port side, I would be joining Marshall."

Story said, "Listen to me and do not ask any questions. Go back, put your plastic dog tag next to Marshall, and bring his to me." Haver did as he was told and handed the blood covered dog tag to Story who wiped it off and told Washington to put it on. "From this moment on, you are Toby Marshall and Haver Washington is dead. I checked Marshals service jacket, he has no relatives and was raised in an orphanage. Haver Washington is wanted for murder back in the states and his wife is not much. You have it all to win and nothing to lose. One important thing I want you to lose is your memory; do not say anything until I tell you to, understand?"

"Right now, I need your help. I was hit in the head with something and I am bleeding all over the place, most important I cannot see. Rap a bandage around my head and read the instruments to me." The new Marshall said, "We are at three thousand feet almost out of gas and the hydraulic pressure on the port side is zero. We are heading due south at two hundred knots." Can you see the field? asked Story. After twenty minutes Marshall said, "Yes sir, straight ahead." Bill said, "Okay, you go around in a slow right turn for a few minutes, turn left and circle the field. Get down to one thousand feet and when you get to the north side get down to two hundred feet. See if the port wheel will come down."

"Now okay, this is the plan. Line up with the center of the runway, put your starboard wheel down, come down to fifty feet, lift your port wing - we do not want it to dig in when we hit the ground. Keep it up as long as you can. Just before we hit, turn off the ignition and push the throttles all the way forward just like you saw them do it in the movies." After the plane slid along a few hundred feet, it came to a halt.

The new Marshall went back to cover-up Stanley and the newly departed Marshall before many people came around. Just then there was an explosion and gasoline from the right wing tank broke the starboard window. This sprayed Bill Story with burning fuel. Marshall grabbed the CO_2 fire extinguisher and after he released his seat belt, he pulled Bill out and put the burning pilot's flight suit fire out. Marshall tore the suit off Story for it was still smoldering. The navy corpsman came and worked on Story, remarking that he was lucky and not too bad. The blood had gotten into his eyes to a point he could not see. The corpsman sprayed Story with something to help his burns and cut away some burnt hair. He then turned to Marshall and said, "Hell, you are worse off then the pilot. You need to go to a hospital right away." Toby's hands were burnt in spite of the heavy gloves.

As Adam was turning his jet to take off for the hospital in Manila, a small private jet cut him off. He stuck his head out the window and called, "Get that plane out of my way. We have wounded aboard." A little man hollered back, "Keep your shirt on old man." Adam asked, "Who is that son of a bitch and what is he doing on this secret base? I will run across that wise guy and we will see who will keep his shirt on."

They landed in Manila where ambulances were waiting and they made good time to the hospital. Bill's head wound was dressed and they cut away a lot of his burnt hair. They said he would be fine in a few days. Marshall, however, was a different story. They said he needed work done on his face and hands right away to prevent infection from setting in. They also said his best chance would be to fly him to Tokyo General because they had larger and better facilities to handle his type of injury.

On the way there, Adam told Bill that plane number two did not make it back. Bill said, "I am not surprised because I saw a mortar shell go off under the plane just before it took off. It may not be too bad as it has a good pilot and a lot of jungle on the way back." Adam said that he would order a seal team to start working in from the coast.

Toby went in for surgery and Collins stopped by to see that Bill that was given a good going over before being released for duty. As Adam was leaving the hospital, the administrator caught up with him and said he would like to see him in his office. The doctor said, "That man you brought in was covered with a white powder that checked out to be one hundred percent heroin." The administrator was Dr. Motto who told Adam that under Japanese law he was required to report it to the police. Adam told him that the man was working undercover to expose a drug ring that was selling drugs to American service men and therefore under military law. The man was in a warehouse where there was a raid and many drugs were spilled. Adam said he understood but if it was reported, it would bring an investigation that would take a lot of paperwork. And because you were the one to turn it in, you would be the main person to take care of it. The doctor thought for a long time and asked, "A lot of paperwork?" Adam said, "Yes indeed." "Maybe our lab made a mistake and it would be better to just forget about the whole thing." answered the doctor. Adam said, "I could not agree more." They shook hands and Adam whistled all the way out of the hospital.

Bill stopped down to see Toby after he came down from surgery. They had operated on his face and would treat his hands starting tomorrow. Bill told Toby that he had to go back to station K to clear up a few things but will be back to check on him again soon.

Adam and Bill flew back to station K and checked with the officer that was in touch with the seal team that reported in every hour. The rest of the crew were back in their service outfits and were given checks for ten thousand dollars each after they reluctantly gave back the bags of bills and coins. They wanted to keep the three gold pieces to remember the mission. Adam said he hoped that they all would forget this mission.

Since the reports from the seal team were coming in every hour, they all said they would like to hang around and all go home together. Adam told them he just found out they all would be raised one grade in rank for completing this mission. That made them happy to hear that. The word arrived that contact was made with the crew of plane two and that all were alive and in good shape. They would be back to base K in twenty-four hours. The whole base celebrated with some beer that seemed to come out of nowhere. Adam remarked, "I can't wait to hear their story, I bet it's a beauty."

Adam said, "Bill, during the Viet Nam war a group from Thailand fought with us with the understanding that once it was over the U.S. would supply them with arms to overthrow their corrupt government back home. The state department made a deal and the navy got the job of carrying it out. We transported arms in and they made a deal to bring out heroin. That was what was in the bales we carried out. Isn't that great? The state department is in the smuggling business!"

"There must have been a leak like there always is of what we were up to. They waited until we delivered that last load of arms and then to get even they turned the mortars against us. The next time state gets in a bind, let them forget the navy and get someone else. We lost two men on this operation and that is two men too many. The planes do not matter because we were going to give them away anyhow. I am really waiting to hear how the plane crew two gets out of the jungle. It was the state department that pushed to get a deal to have everybody get a higher rate increase. Incidentally, you are now a captain in the United States Navy. Congratulations Captain Story."

Bill said, "You know Admiral Collins has a nice ring to it." Adam smiled and said "Yes, it does and while we are waiting I have a story of my own. Can I get dispensation first for confessing to an admiral? Is it the same as confessing to a priest?" Adam looked at Bill and said" I am not falling for that old dodge but I will listen and give you penance later." Bill started, "First, Bill Manning arrested Washington back at B base on charges that he murdered someone back in the states before he enlisted in the navy. His wife is seven months pregnant and was blackmailing Washington for more money. She turned him in when he refused to pay after he found out about the baby. He was last home over a year ago so you can see the picture. When Marshall got his head blown off we switched dog tags. Marshall had no relatives and was brought up in an orphanage. I also told him to lose his memory until we could figure this out."

Adam said, "What do you mean 'WE'? You already figured out I would go along with this plan." After a few seconds Adam looked Bill in the eye and said, "Do you think we can away with it?"

Bill said, "They sure as hell can't fingerprint Washington now. Washington is now Marshall, so Haver is now Toby. The best part of the story is that his mother in-law was blackmailing him and making him have sex with her two-three times a week and wanted him to screw her sister who lives next door. He was worried because she had two more sisters down the street. I had to shoot the lock off the makeshift jail to get him out. Manning ran and left him locked up. His lovely wife will get the insurance money and live happy ever after. Toby will be over here for a long time getting his hands repaired from the burns he got saving my life."

Bill took care of the paperwork to send the bodies of Washington and Moore home along with their belongings and checks for ten thousand dollars. Their wives will get a hundred thousand from the service member's insurance also. He regretted sending any money to Washington's wife after the way she treated him but it ends that part of his life that makes the plan work

The crew of plane two arrived, cleaned up, and was having some chow before coming out to tell everybody their story on how they got back. When they were all set, they sat down and told their story in detail. The explosion that Story saw was the beginning of all their headaches. It took out their oil line to the port engine and all the hydraulics to the controls. The pilot said he could keep the plane just above the tree tops for awhile, maybe thirty minutes. Then the starboard engine quit. They were lucky to find a small clearing to set the plane down but it was not very long and the plane ran out of clearing and went crashing into the jungle. Right after takeoff they all knew they were in trouble so they strapped themselves in tight that ended up saving their lives. Right after they got out of the plane a band of natives surrounded the plane carrying rifles. They thought they were finished. The head man stepped out and to our surprise; it was a white man with an Australian accent - why he was there with those of natives, we do not know. He went into the plane as the natives kept us under guard. When he came out, we offered him the money that you gave us to bribe our way home. He started to laugh and said he did not want our money but would trade our freedom for our cargo. We thought that was a fair exchange; the damned stuff did not belong to us anyway. He was happy and sent a few natives to guide us to the coast. As soon as they saw the seals coming, they disappeared into the bush. We do not know what was in the cargo, but it saved our lives.

Collins laughed and said, "It was worth more then you think. As soon as you give us back the bribe money,

I will give you all a check for ten thousand dollars as a bonus. Transportation has been arranged."

"Oh yes, I almost forgot. You have been given a promotion to the next highest grade. Please remember, this was a secret mission and any mention of it will result in court martial."

The two remaining planes were stripped of their instruments and the planes were given away to a local airline. Before they left Bill and Adam emptied Toby's sea bag on to a table. They were completely surprised with the contents. There were bales of money, some U.S., some Japanese. There were bank books from Tokyo and Hawaii; almost a hundred of them. Adam said, "If you fly enough in this area you can smuggle things out of some of these backward areas and sell them on the black market and make a fortune." Toby was going to retire from the navy a very rich man. There were also papers showing he had two storage lockers in Tokyo and with the power of attorney from Toby, they made arrangements to pick up what ever they contained. Adam said, "Now that I am an admiral, I can ship them to an office at North Island California." Bill stopped in to see Toby before going home. Bill said, "Toby, I retired once a commander and now as a captain." Toby said he was being transferred to the Naval Hospital in San Diego and would see him there. Toby was now a chief petty officer.

Bill was back in the real estate business and Willa was happy to have him around again. Willa was taking Laura to college, which was four hours away. On the way home, a truck driver blinded by the sun drove her into a guardrail and she was sent to a hospital. Bill was called and he called Laura to tell her that her mother had been in an accident and to get transportation to the local hospital. He would meet her there. Bill got there and saw that Laura, who had gotten there before him, had been crying. The situation must be very bad. Willa was unconscious with tubes running out of all parts of her body. Hours went by and after what seemed like gallons of coffee; Bill fell asleep in the emergency room. He dreamed of Willa meeting him as he got off the plane at North Island Naval Air Station when he got in from Hawaii. She turned to Adam and said, "Thank you for bringing him back like you said you would. He looks like he spent the last two months on some Pacific island somewhere." Bill turned to Adam and laughed.

He remembered Willa saying, "I have the most beautiful vacation planed. Since we have spent the most of our lives in the western part of the country I thought it would be nice to go to the other coast for a change. The place is Paradise Island just off the east coast, a short hop form Miami. It has everything - white sandy beaches and the nightlife there is dancing right next to the casino." They took off the next day and found that it was everything the brochure said it was. They did not get out of bed the first day except to put the 'do not disturb' sign on the door. They made love all day long; Willa was as great as he remembered. They danced and tried their luck at the casino. Bill lay in bed the next morning and said he could spend the rest of his life there but all things have to end. Laura was going to college so they had to go back to help her pack and get her things together.

Bill felt a hand on his knee and woke up to reality. There was a doctor with Laura. Laura spoke first. "Dad, mom did not make it." The doctor explained to Bill that there was too much damage to support her. Bill said, "This does not make sense - I go away for months at a time and everything is fine. I retire and stay home and then I lose my wife." Bill said to himself, "Oh god, what am I going to do now?" Laura kissed her father and said, "Dad, we will work everything out and it will be fine." Then they both went in to see Willa. The tubes were gone and she looked at peace. Bill thought that she looked like she was asleep and questioned whether she was really gone.

Willa's funeral was the largest the area could remember. Willa had belonged to a great number of organizations mainly because Bill was way so much and she had so much free time. Bill was well-liked in the navy so they were very well represented. Willa's parents were grief stricken, losing their only child this way.

Bill tried to get himself together by getting back to work, but seeing Willa's parents everyday was very hard to take. The thing that amazed him was the way the word got around that this retired navy pilot was now single. The phone was ringing off the wall by women that wanted to be taken around to look at houses. They are willing to pay anything he asked for a house. The old saying must be true 'the woman buys the house but it is the man who pays for it'. A man does not give a damn as long as his wife lets him play golf every day." Willa's parents sold the real estate business and moved to Del Mar Cliffs overlooking the ocean. Bill did not have to work, for when his parents came west; they bought up land for a song before the west started to develop.

Bill was cleaning out his desk went a car pulled up out front and out stepped out a tall black man. He stopped to read the sign out front and then let himself in to an almost empty office. He heard a sound from one of the offices and went back to see who was there. He knocked on the doorframe and Bill looked up. He said, "The office is closed and the business had been sold. Can I help you in any way?" The black man said, "You do not know me do you?" Bill looked at him a little longer and said "Toby, you old son of a gun you look great."

Toby said," I am so sorry that you lost your wife and after all you went through over seas." Asked what he was up to, Toby said "You are not going to believe this but I went back to my old neighborhood. My wife was working in the same store, but this time on day shift. I walked in bought a few things - we were two feet apart when she checked me out but she did not recognize me. I hung around outside for awhile until I saw this man come down the street with a little girl. It must have been the end of Sherry's shift for she ran out and kissed this person and the little girl. This must have been the child she was expecting while I was overseas. I looked at this person and thought I recognized him. This is the son of a bitch I was supposed to have killed that night we had a fight, however, he looked very alive to me. I hope they enjoy all my money and hope he enjoys screwing his wife's old woman and all of her sisters too. I was not out of boot camp when that bastard was crawling into bed with Sherry."

"I almost forgot," said Toby, Admiral Collins wants to see us both tomorrow in his office over at North Island, at 0900." Bill said he would be there.

At 0900, Bill and Toby walked into the admiral's office and after a few cups of coffee; they went into a backroom. Adam left word with his yeoman that they were not to be disturbed. Adam got a crow bar and handed it to Toby who said, "With these hands - no thank you." Adam took the crowbar, opened up number one, and then gave them orders to take an account of just what they contained. He peeled a cloth back. Adam said, "Oh my, there must be thousands of Japanese bank notes worth maybe a million dollars here. I wonder what he sold to get this much money." They opened up the second one and there they found it was full of porcelain vases and figurines. "These are probably hundreds of years old. That is where he made so much money, smuggling ancient heirlooms out of the backcountry to markets in Japan. Flying out of China, Cambodia and Viet Nam over the years as an aircrew member was no trouble at all." The third and forth chest held silver bars and porcelain dolls in rare silks so no wonder they were so heavy.

Collins said, "The bank notes and bank accounts are no problem, but the rest will take some doing. I know some people that can help us out and will take most of this for a fat commission. "Bill, can we store this stuff out at your place? We cannot keep it here on the base, suppose they pull an inspection." Bill said, "Why not use the same system that was used in Tokyo - put it in a storage space. Adam said, "Well, my chief, Casey has a pick up we can use; it will not look good for a navy vehicle backing up to a storage place. Bill said, "We could use false names." Bill said, "I have many dead relatives who will not mind us using their names." They found a storage area not far away and all three were given identification cards and keys. Adam said, "I will make some calls tomorrow about the contents of the chests."

Bill said that he was thinking about giving his bonus check to Stanley's widow as she has two small children to raise. Adam agreed he would go along with it too. Toby said, "I have so much money so how about I give a hundred thousand." Adam said he would take care of the checks in the morning. Adam's chief petty officer tracked down Stanley's address and Bill and Adam headed out into the hills to Riverside California the next day.

After a three-hour drive, they found the house that Stanley had described to Bill on the long flights over the Pacific. His wife answered the door. She was as beautiful as Stanley said. Trailing on her apron strings were two children - a boy and a girl. "Come in." she said, "please have a seat. I recognized you both from the letters Stanley sent home. I want you to meet my children, Ann and Stanley Jr." She gave them her apron and asked them to take it out to the kitchen. Adam told her there was some money coming from an unofficial source that cannot be divulged. She thanked them and had a good idea where the money came from. As they were leaving Admiral Collins gave her one of his cards and said "If there is anything you need at all please give me a call." She said that she would and thanked them as they left. On the way home, they stopped for dinner and over a drink agreed that it had been a nice thing to do and it made them feel good.

Willa's parents moved to a nice home on a cliff overlooking the Pacific not too far away. This would be a nice place for Laura to spend some time in the summer. The older folks can sit on the porch, look out over the water and try to forget the horrible last two months.

Bill was getting antsy around the house - after all how many times can you polish the car? When the phone rang, it was Adam who just gotten back from Washington. Adam asked Bill to have dinner with him – "It will be on me so pick out a nice expensive place." Bill said, "Remember the last time you asked me out to dinner, it almost got me killed in some far off country that nobody gave a shit about." Adam said," I will buy you the biggest lobster you can find." Bill accepted and said, "Okay, pick me up at seven." Bill was waiting at the curb - anything to get him out of the house and around people again. They went to the El Coronado and had the lobster that Adam had been talking about. Bill said, "I'll bet you're on a huge expense account this time to pay for lobster that big."

Adam, "Do you remember Hale McClour?" "He was my wingman there for a while back in the good old days when we flew in Viet Nam. His in-laws persuaded him to run for the governor of Pennsylvania; you know he was a navy hero and all that and damned if he was not elected. He went on to be elected to be president of the United States." Bill said, "I never made the connection." Adam continued, "I just came back from meeting with him. We walked around in the rose garden, the only place he feels safe. He thinks the whole place is bugged. Nobody trusts anyone in Washington any more."

"He wants me to be the drug czar, head of the drug enforcement department. The war on drugs is a big joke and nobody is doing anything about it. I told him that I would take the job on two conditions. First, I pick my own team of experts with no interference or pressure from Washington and second to do the job and win. He told me that nobody knows it yet, but he is not running for another term but to 'keep that under your hat'. "This place is a bunch of idiots and I let them think I am going to run again so they think they can control me. I have more money then I can ever spend so who needs this job?"

He continued to tell me, "Your budget will come from money the party stashed away over the years that I just found out about from a senator who retired. They cannot do a thing about it because it is illegal and too many big names are attached to it. I have copies of everything in good hands so they dare not shoot me. Pick all the people you need from any source. If you need the armed forces you've got them. I will send out letters tomorrow to tell them to give you complete cooperation. All agencies military and civilian will have these letters in two days. Any problem, call me at this private line."

"Then he gave me his card."

Adam said, "I have started to get a good group together, but I need a right hand man to be my executive officer, just like the last time." Bill said, "This time I hope they don't start shooting at me. The last time I damned near burnt alive and I would have if it was not for Toby – remember?" Adam said, "Oh, nothing like that this time, all you have to do is flying around a lot. Bill asked, "A lot of flying? Ummm." Adam nodded and Bill said, "You got your self an exec."

Adam told him to meet him at a place down by the docks in a restaurant called the Moving On, and to wear old clothes and try not look too smart. Adam dropped him off and said, "See if you can find the place for breakfast at ten." Bill got there early to make sure he could find the place. All those around the place seem to be dockworkers or truck drivers. It did not look too much of a place but he waited until ten and went inside. There was Adam with two other men. He was introduced to George Beck and Mark Kent. Just then a loud-mouth redhead waitress showed up - big tits and an ass to match wearing much too much lipstick and eye make up. Bill could not keep his eyes off her. She stuck her tits in Bill's direction and said "Hi there handsome, see any thing you like?" She kidded with the entire blue-collar crowd and insulted them as much as they did her. She showed up with Bill's breakfast of hot cakes and bacon along with coffee then left saying, "See you later sweetie."

This old bag insulted Bill and he did not like it. The men told him her name was Dixie and when all the men teased her about her protruding ass, she would come back with, 'you only wish you could afford it honey'. Bill did not being called 'sweetie' in front of other men but Adam said to be a good sport and to leave a nice tip.

When they left, they did not go out to the parking lot as he expected, but went around back to a lower level. They went in a back door and inside there was a long table like you would see in a company boardroom. The seats on both sides of the table were full and Adam was seated at the far end. At the near end were two seats, so Bill sat there to see what would happen. In a few minutes a young woman came in and everybody stood up. As they sat down she turned to Bill and said, "Hi there sweetie, did you enjoy you hot cakes?" Everybody laughed and Adam spoke to Bill, "Let me introduce you to Dixie from upstairs." Bill was dumfounded. Here was a beautiful lady not at all like the one upstairs. His face turned blood red and this was the second time today she embarrassed him and made him feel uncomfortable. Adam began, "Okay, we all know Dixie so let's have everybody introduce themselves starting on the right." The men stood up and started: George Beck, customs; Henry Green, AFT; Hal Ladan, coast guard; Mark Kent, border patrol; Roger Ralston, naval intelligence; Brad Wilson, U.S. Marines; Will Milford, U.S. Army; Louis

Newman, N.S.A; Woody Miner, California State Police. The last person introduced herself, Lt. Sara West, naval intelligence.

Adam said "This is Bill Story, my executive officer." "Any time you can't get a hold of me whatever Bill says, it is as if it comes directly from me. We operate as a unit - no secrets, no competition and we share every thing we know or find out amongst ourselves. Use your informants, if you do not have any, get some. The best way to find out what is going on in a town is to ask a cab driver as they get to know everybody's business. Hotel door attendants know who is coming and who is going and they get cabs for people at hotels. They also hear where the cabbie is told to go. Recruit as many as you can, we have a large budget." "Bill, this group is known as the board of directors; we will meet again in two weeks.

Adam turned to Bill and said, "Dixie can find out more information in one day than we can pick up in weeks. Those truckers travel all over the country and like to sit around and talk to one another. They do not pay any attention to Dixie as she is just the one that takes their orders and brings the food. They treat her like a piece of furniture and talk freely in front of her. Listening is a science and we do not have the training to do a good job at it; we are good at flying planes and that is our trade."

"Members of the board have jobs besides working for us and may have to leave those jobs at a moments notice. If they catch hell for leaving those jobs, call me and I will made it right. Next week, a letter from the president is going out to all agencies informing the military to give us full cooperation. Our job is to stop the smuggling of narcotics into and around our county."

"Bill, I hope you will join us as my executive officer. It requires a lot of flying."

"That is like putting candy in front of a child," Bill said, "and in that case you've got yourself a man."

"We bend the rules to do this job and maybe it is the rules that make the war on drugs impossible to succeed in the first place."

"Woody Miner will contact all the state police agencies in the country to be able to talk to one another at all times using their computers. We meet again in two weeks. "Any questions?" "No?" "Okay, the meeting is adjourned. Would Miner, Beck, and Green please stay for a few minutes?"

"Here is the drill. If you see a drug kingpin, pull him over on a minor offence and tell him he has a broken tail light. Run him in and before his lawyer gets there raising hell to get him out, photograph everything in his car. Pay a lot of attention to the glove box, trunk, and under the seat. Be careful to put everything back just as it was, making sure of course, that he really did have a broken tail light - all before he gets out. That was what I meant about bending the rules to get things done, understand?"

Bill Story gave out cards with new phone numbers, which said they were morticians, which was a nice touch.

Tucked away in the hills of Pennsylvania outside of the little town of Elysburg is a very private boys' school named Fort Lee. The school has an excellent scholastic record. Their graduates go on to be leaders in the military, politics, and industry. The school has no sports at all, no football, no baseball no basketball as all efforts go into preparing the students for their successes in life. One of the seniors is Richard McClour, son of the president of the United States, who is not there by the wishes of the board of trustees. He is there because his mother's family is the largest donor to the school's budget. The school does not like the security people around in the classroom or in the room where the students sleep. Richard is the product of money and gets his own way most of the time. His mother bought him a B.M.W. which is against the rules for a student to have at school. She said that it was just for riding around the campus. However, he would sneak out at night and run into town for pizza. On his eighteenth birthday one of his security people ran him into town to get his drivers license and on the way back to school he was stopped doing eighty in a forty-mile limit zone. The officer, when he found out who he had stopped, stepped back and let him off. "See" the little bastard told Norm Patterson, his security guard, "When they find out who I am, they are afraid of my parents."

Back in San Diego Bill Story and Adam Collins took off from North Island Air Station heading south along the Baja. Bill said," I hate to mention this but we are in Mexican waters."

"That's okay; we have permission to fly off their coast in the search of smugglers." Adam said. "This plane is too small and tomorrow we will come back in a larger plane with one of those new cameras I have read about."

The next morning they came out with a larger plane with the new cameras and this time they had a photographer's mate first class. They had a camera on each side of the plane so that way they did not have to move the camera for going down and coming back. "Okay, Pete, "Are you all loaded up with plenty of film and ready to go?"

"Yes sir, plenty off coffee and sandwiches too."

"Good man." replied Adam. "I want you to take pictures of everything that floats and the full coast line down and back."

"Yes sir." - which is the only answer you give to an admiral.

Adam said, "I want to see what you have by 0900 tomorrow."

When they returned from the flight, Bill and Adam showered and sat down to a meal on the base. The advantage of having quarters on the base is that you can eat well and fly in and out without having to drive back and forth. At dinner in the Flying Could restaurant, Adam said to Bill "I have a surprise for you. Toby is taking flying lessons. He said he cannot work on them, but he can learn to fly them."

Bill said "Who do you think flew my plane back to station K on the last flight return? He flew in and landed on one wheel. Too bad he could not have gotten a medal for that. The trouble with medals is they have to backed-up by paper records and when Toby was in the hospital in Tokyo, they found heroin all over him."

Bill said," I thought that was what we were hauling." Adam said, "You know how those doctors hate paperwork. He said that by law he had to report it but changed his mind when I reminded him of the paperwork he would have to do so he said he must have been mistaken."

In the morning, after breakfast, they went over to operations to look at the pictures they had taken yesterday to see if anything was worth taking a second look. There were hundreds of pictures of vessels – large and small, complete coverage of the shoreline and as they turned the pages one caught Bill's eye. "Ho! turn that last one back."

Bill asked Pete if he could blow that one up to a point where they could see the name of the ship. Pete said, "Be back in five minutes." He returned and spread the large page out on the desk. Bill asked Adam if he saw something he recognized. At first, Adam did not see anything familiar. Then it hit him. "That looks like the ship that was in port at station K. It is the Pagan Island - booms forward and amidships and the wheelhouse leaning forward."

"Pete can you tell us just when you took this picture?"

"Sure, Mister Story, all the pictures are numbered in the order they were taken. This picture was taken about half way through the flight."

Adam picked up the phone and called his chief. "Casey, get me Hal Ladan at the coast guard and have him call here at operations."

The phone rang and the petty officer handed it to Adam. "Hal, there is a vessel headed north and it's just south off the Baja going at a pretty good rate. The name is the Pagan Island. See what you can find out about it and get back to me here."

The information came back after one cup of coffee.

"The ownership is hard to determine but it is slated to tie up at pier one In San Diego at 0800, Thursday."

Adam turned to Bill and remarked, "That is less then forty-eight hours from now." He had to get busy.

At Fort Lee, the security people flipped to see who was going to be the lucky one to ride with Richard McClour back to Washington after the graduation that neither parent attended. Momma wanted her son away far enough not to interfere with her social functions.

Bill Patterson lost and he rode shotgun all the way back. Little Richard was doing ninety on two lane roads and Norm was hoping for the police to pull him over so he could take over the wheel but no such luck.

When Patterson got to the White House, he told Maxwell Chase, the head of security, that he would not ride with that crazy kid again. "That crazy kid is going to kill someone and I do not want to be that person. He drives ninety in a forty mile an hour zone. At school, we took parts off his car so he could not drive it. Hell, he sent into town and had a man come out and put new parts on."

Maxwell said, "The boy likes you. In fact he wants you to ride with him down to a rally down in Virginia on Saturday."

"Oh, no - I told you I will not ride with him again."

Max said, "No problem. We will have a car in front of you and two in back. This will be an easy ride but get some maps in case you have to change routes."

Driving out with security in front and rear, they left the White House in a nice slow pace but things changed as soon as they hit Virginia. Richard slowed and let the car in front get ahead and then turned left and out-ran the heavy security agents' cars. They could not keep up with him. Patterson was turning green going at such a speed. They got to the rally in Warrenton, Virginia, ten minutes before the security people. When they got there Bill handed Maxwell the keys to Richard's car and said, "Get someone else to ride back with him - I want to live a little longer:"

Patterson turned to Maxwell and after handing him the keys to the B.M.W. and said, "I will never again ride with that crazy son of a bitch. He drives ninety miles an hour on a two lane road posted at forty. He has a death wish and I don't want any part of it."

Maxwell Chase said that he would get someone else - someone with some guts, to ride back to Washington with Richard.

"Your job is to follow orders and you will report to my office; maybe then we will decide your future with this agency." said Max. Patterson answered, "Max, that kid is on something. When I looked into his eyes, there was nobody home."

Max said," You are suspended as of now. The two men that were assigned to guard little Richard will follow him everywhere he goes."

That should be easy, because Patterson had him dress in an orange Baltimore Oriole jacket and a white ball cap. Richard and the agents walked around for awhile before Richard said he needed a restroom. The gents wanted to go in the restroom with him, but Richard said, "Good god, can't I even take a leak without you standing by my side?" One of the agents went inside and looked around and found the only other way out was small window ten feet up the back wall. The agent said, "Okay go, but we will be waiting right here.'

About ten minutes went by before Richard came out. He led the agents down toward the bandstand where they were setting up to start playing. One agent said to the other, "Did you think Richard was that tall?"

They got to the boy in the Oriole jacket and turned him around and said, "Oh my god, this isn't Richard! Where did you get that jacket and hat?"

The boy said, "Some boy came in the men's room and we smoked some pot before he gave me fifty dollars to change clothes, put on these glasses, and walk down to the band stand. "Hey!", "fifty bucks is pretty good just to walk down to the band stand. He said it was to fool his girl friend!"

The agents ran back to where Maxwell and Patterson were still standing and told them they lost Richard. "He gave us the slip. What is his mother going to say?"

Patterson answered, "We have a bigger problem than that - his car is gone too!"

Just then, they heard police sirens out toward the highway. Max hollered to Patterson, "Hop in the car with me." They did not go very far before they came upon the worst scene possible. There was a red sports car smashed into a tree and the president's son was twenty-five feet from the car. Patterson thought to himself - I said that kid was out to kill someone and it turned out to be himself. Maxwell went over to the sergeant in charge and identified himself. He said "That young man is the son of the president of the United States and we have to move fast before the press comes snooping around. Take the tags off, give them to me, get a tow truck to tow the car to a secure area down at the station, and cover it up. We do not want anyone around taking pictures, Okay?"

When the ambulance showed up, Maxwell went over to the two medics and said, "This young man is the president's son, and he showed them his identification. Put him the ambulance and drive to the main entrance to the Arlington Cemetery. You will meet a navy ambulance there and you'll transfer the body to it. They will take it from there."

Maxwell got the two police officers and the two medics together and gave each one a hundred dollar bill. Just then, a state police officer showed up and Maxwell repeated the same facts and gave him a hundred dollar bill also. "Local officers cannot move out of the county, but you can. Please escort the ambulance quietly to the main entrance of the Arlington Cemetery where you will meet a navy ambulance. They will take over from there. Please keep all of this under your hat and I will see all of you in a few days and make it worth your while.

"Tell your captain," he told the medics, "that I will take care of the station house later and to keep a lid on it."

"Again, I ask you to keep this quiet. We all would like the first family to hear this from my office rather than to read about it in the newspaper. A call that their only child has had a fatal accident is bad enough coming from an office in the White House but getting the call from some reporter looking for a story would be much worse."

Richard's body was taken to the Bethesda Naval Hospital and rushed into a private area where doctors examined the young man. Maxwell Chase told the necessary people to prepare the family for the shock that goes with this type of news.

On the way back to the white house, Max turned to Patterson and said, "I should have listened to you when you told me the boy was a menace to himself and others. I feel guilty for not doing things a lot differently."

The president's minister and top White House security people were there to help the family get through this delicate time. There were people there to keep others out of the room and to give the family time to digest the recent turn of events. A doctor from the Naval Hospital told the family that Richard died of a broken neck and that death was instantaneous. There would be no autopsy but blood samples were taken and the results would be shared only with the family.

The next week Maxwell went to the bank after making some phone calls and at three in the afternoon he went to the volunteer firehouse in Warrenton, Virginia. There he met all the people that were at the accident scene. Max said that it was great that they did not let the word of the accident get out and he then handed envelopes to each one and also gave one to the medic to give to the captain of the fire station. He offered his thanks again, turned, and walked away. Each man opened up his envelope and found in it ten one hundred dollar bills. They called the captain in and handed him what Maxwell had given them to give to the firehouse. Inside was a check for ten thousand dollars.

The president was visibly depressed after Richard was buried in the family plot in Pennsylvania in a private service. That kept the reporters away and the best they could do was take some long distance photographs. From the information they received, the best they could come up with was to report that the president's son died of a heart attack

Adam had to cancel the next board meeting due to flying to Washington to meet with the president. He got to the oval office early, for like so many they are used to cooling their heels outside and waiting. To his surprise, as soon as the president heard he was there, he came right out and directed him to the Rose Garden. That is the place where the president felt comfortable to talk to Adam.

I know what happened to Richard and I am glad no one else was hurt in the accident. He probably got the drugs from his mother's room. Do not look so surprised. Merna has been on drugs for years. She has been in hospitals all over the world under different names. Try running for office with that little bit of information hanging over your head. That is one reason I will not run for re-election. The other is that Washington is full of people waiting for you to make even the smallest error. I have more money than I can ever spend. Maybe Merna and I should go to some small island where there are no drugs. He smiled and said, "Hell she would probably smoke the coconuts."

"As long as they think I will run again they figure they have me by the ass. What will they do when word leaks out that I am spending all the money I found that they had squirreled away in illegal accounts? The party hopefuls never had any idea I would find those accounts and I would not have if Senator Butler hadn't told me just before he died last year. I have been waiting for a cause to spend it on and now it is all yours. They cannot touch me on this as there are too many names connected to this money. I have letters in several different safe deposit boxes that if any thing happens to me, their ass is mud."

"A new letter is going out tomorrow to all agencies that states you will have their full cooperation or else. Adam, spend the money to do whatever you need to get the job done. I will be in office for another two years and any request you submit will be honored."

Adam laughed to himself all the way back to the west coast thinking this was going to piss a lot of people off. The president is going to close off the borders and is increasing the coast guard's budget five hundred percent.

Adam called a board meeting told them about his meeting with the president. "We have the money and his full cooperation; nothing is going to stop us now. First thing we have to do is stop the Pagan Island from docking and unloading when we are sure that it is carrying a large shipment of heroin. This ship will be tied up at pier one where it can unload directly on to flat bed trucks. We have a plan to throw a monkey wrench into their plans. We will tie something up to pier one to preventing them from unloading until we are ready for them to do so. We will get an entomologist to inspect the cargo and he will find insect eggs and parts that will require the cargo of rice, destined for Food Hunger Relief Organization in Saint Louis, to be cleansed."

"Henry Green, you and your men get to looking into this organization right away and hire as many as you need. Need money, call me. Mark Kent, get with Will Milford and see how many men he needs to help at the borders. The army is trained and they will fit in fine. Put a new man with a veteran and it will work out fine. George Beck, get your people to hunt down an entomologist in this area and get him here by tomorrow morning mentioning that all expenses including his pay will be covered. Woody Miner, get with all law enforcement agencies to start to put pressure on all roads – small and interstates. I want all suspicious cars and trucks stopped, pulled over, and inspected no matter who is driving them. If the smuggling is being done by blacks, pull them over, if is Hispanics, pull them over. I will handle the press that is sure to raise hell if we pull over minorities. When you can use minorities to help out, that may soften the situation somewhat. Coast Guard Hal Ladan, work with N.S.A. and Louis Newman to map out all ships heading this way - where they are going, where they came from, and what their cargos are. Naval Intelligence Roger Ralston, work with Dixie and collect all the information you can; we need it."

"Let's go, meeting adjourned." Adam called his chief petty officer and told him to call over to the naval shipyard and tell the man in charge that he will be over there in two hours.

Adam, Bill, and George Beck joined them for lunch; they had to talk things over.

"George did you get the bug doctor I asked for?" The reply was," Yes sir, he will be here tomorrow morning and will have samples of the bugs you asked for. He will be at your offices at the downtown Hilton early."

Bill and Adam left, drove over to the shipyard, and on the way Adam said, "We have to tie up pier one somehow."

As they entered the yard, they were challenged at the gate. Adam showed the petty officer his I.D.card, got a proper salute and was asked if he would like an escort. "No." said Adam, "I think I can find my way."

They headed towards the tallest building and inside seated at a desk was a young lady, a petty officer second-class. Adam asked, "Who is your commanding officer and where can I find him this minute?" She replied, "His name is Commander Bill Wilson and he cannot be disturbed as he is in a meeting."

Adam said, "Where is he?" "The second door on the right?" "Thank you." Bill opened the door and he and Adam walked in. The room was full of naval officers and civilian supervisors around a large table. The commander at the far end of the table stood up and asked, "Who are you and what right do you have breaking up my meeting?" Adam answered, "I know who I am and you should too since you were told that I would be here in two hours. Well, the two hours are up. My name is Admiral Adam Collins and my aide is Commander Story."

Commander Wilson's face got red and he said, "I thought that was for tomorrow."

"Sloppy organization wouldn't you say, Mister Story?" said Adam turning to Bill.

"Yes sir, and maybe the next time you are in Washington you should mention it, Admiral."

The commander was hooked. "What can I do for you Admiral?"

Adam replied, "I need something, a ship or a barge, to be tied up to pier one in two hours and it is to remain there until I ask to have it moved.

The commander said, "That pier belongs to the city and I cannot tie it up".

"Mister Story, did not he say he will do anything I asked."

"Yes sir, admiral, he sure did."

Wilson said, "Sir, it will be done"

Before Adam left Commander Wilson's office he said, "You probably did not see the last letter that came out." as he pulled it from his pocket and handed it to the commander. "Do you recognize the signature at the bottom?" The commander nearly crapped himself, as it was signed by the president himself. He then said, "Admiral, anything you need, just call."

"Bill, let's eat at the Moving On tonight so you can watch Dixie's ass as she works." Adam thought it was funny, but Bill did not. As they sat there later waiting to be helped, two men were engaged in an intense argument and they were going at it hot and heavy. When Dixie came to their table she asked, "Hi sailors, see anything you like?" Adam damned near fell off his chair. Bill's face turned red like it always did.

Adam asked, "Dixie, who are those two men that seemed to be mad at each other?"

She said, "The one in uniform is the port captain and the other is congressman Caesar Markos, a big wheel around here." Adam said, "I have seen that well-dressed man before but can't remember where or when." After a few moments he said, "That's the little son of a bitch that cut us off when I was trying to take off at station K. He told me to keep my shirt on and I am waiting to get him to keep his shirt on. I will fix his wagon one day, wait and see."

"Let's go down to the pier after dinner and see what is going on." When they got there, they found flat-bed trucks backed up waiting for the Pagan Island to tie up. Just then Pete Marcona, the port captain, shows up and asked, "Why is that old barge still tied up here? It is blocking the way for the ship coming in at 0800 tomorrow."

Adam said, "There are other piers; why not use one of them?" Marcona said, "This is the only pier where the ship that has its own cranes can unload directly on to flat bed trucks."

"Well," answered Adam, "there must be an emergency for the navy to tie up here and it will probably move in a day or two."

Adam and Bill went over to his office at the Hilton where they met Woody Miner, state police; George Beck, customs; and Brad Wilson, marines. Adam told them, "I want the marines to wear plain coveralls and help with truck inspection."

Roger Ralston found the old grain-drying plant out on Route Four and talked the owner into renting it to them for a week or so. He was glad to accommodate them but warned them it was bad shape. Moreover, it would take some work to get it working. Adam said," Get it open and we will do the rest."

"Bill, get on the horn to Wilson over at the yard and tell him to keep the barge tied up at pier one until he hears from me and also tell him that one of my people will stop over in an hour and pick up two of his best engineers. We have an old grain-drying plant to get in shape in a few days. We will also need welders, pipe fitters, boilermakers, and a company of shore patrol for security. He needs to have the entire group ready to go as soon as you get there in order for you to lead the convoy in one hour. You had better get moving."

Roger said, "We are going to need some backs as the place is a mess. Okay, call the commanding officer over at the boot camp; I am sure he will lend us a couple hundred men for a week or so."

Bill got hold of the chief pretty officer in charge of the shore patrol and told him he wanted the area secure as soon as possible and also to set up a mess tent. Hard workers need good hot food.

The next morning Adam met with the entomologist at the Hilton where Adam rented rooms for all his workers. The doctor introduced himself as James Q. Adams. Adam laughed and said, "So as not to be confused from now on, you are called Jimmy, okay?"

"Hell, Adam, I have been called a lot worse then that."

Bill showed up with Roger and George and all were introduced to Jimmy. Adam said, "This is the plan. We let them unload most of the cargo and have the trucks move over into the truck inspection area. Jimmy will take samples of the rice and find it contaminated, with insect eggs and bug parts. That okay with you Jim?"

"Hell, Adam, if we can keep these drugs off the streets I will swear it has elephant dung in it."

The next morning Adam met with the port captain and an agent for the Pagan Island. He apologized and said the navy will probably move the barge shortly, maybe tomorrow before noon. Meanwhile the Pagan Island was anchored across the harbor near the north island shore. The agent for the ship said, as requested, he checked into the ownership of the ship and found that it had been leased to a company that was no longer in business. It had no other history so it did not seem to belong to anybody. Bill went down to the docks and saw the flat trucks waiting for their ship to come over so they could be loaded and be on their way. They were paid by the mile so sitting around was costing them money

While Bill was there, he stopped in to see Dixie and have some breakfast. As she was taking his order, she leaned down and said, "They are going to move the barge away from pier one tomorrow morning." He wondered how she knew about it before he did. Adam called over to the shipyard to the commander, asked him to please move the barge tonight, and thanked him for doing a fine job.

Adam met with Jimmy, George Beck, and Brad Wilson. He said, "This is the way we have it planned. After most of the trucks are loaded and are inspected by the state police and the marines, Jimmy here will do his job of inspecting the rice and finding insect eggs ant parts. He will order all the rice to be heated over at the grain cleansing plant on Route Four."

Bill called Adam and said he needed lift trucks to move the rice bags in and out of the plant.

Adam told him to call Wilson over at the yard and he would send anything he wanted.

After that they met at the Hilton for a seafood dinner. Bill was not one to shy away from a free meal.

At dinner Adam said, "Jimmy here is the one that will make our plan work. The inspectors will tie the trucks up so that none of them can get permission to go out on the road."

After a large meal, they all retired for the night. The next morning they met at the dock where the ship was loading the flat-bedded trucks. Just as the last trucks were being loaded, Jimmy came over with his probe and started to sample the rice bags. Just then, the port captain and Congressional Representative Markos came over and to ask what he was doing? Jimmy showed them his credentials and said that he was licensed to inspect any cargo coming into this country. "You have to be very careful you know. Remember what happened when a boy brought a peach in from Italy and it cost the government billions to get rid of the fruit fly? It is time the birds over in Washington got wise."

Markos said, "They never inspected our food before; all of this rice is going to charity "

Jimmy pulled his probe out from a bag of rice and emptied it on a white cloth; there were bug eggs and insect parts. He said, "Look at this," and as he held it in front of the two, their eyes got as big as saucers. "Oh my," said Jimmy, "not only will the whole cargo have to be heated to kill any insects and their eggs but the ship has to be fumigated. I will call the proper agency to take care of the ship while the rice is being cleansed."

All trucks were routed over to the cleansing plant on Route Four to unload. Markos and the port captain knew the jig was up; they would find the drugs as soon as they opened the bags of rice.

At the cleansing plant, they found plastic bags inside the rice bags, two or more were found in each rice container. The drugs they found were starting to overflow the metal handcarts to the point they stacked them over in the corner. Adam told the marine in charge to keep a good eye on the bags of dope over in the corner as we do not want any of this stuff to be carried away.

Adam was watching the operation when his phone rang. It was the security guard at the front gate and he was having trouble with a man who wanted to see the person in charge. Adam told him he would be right up. When he got to the gate he met a man all dressed up who said he was an aide to congressional representative Markos. Adam introduced himself and asked the man's business. The man said the congressional representative was demanding that every thing that was taken off the ship be given back to the proper owner, which was the World Hunger Organization. The man showed Adam his government I.D. Unimpressed Adam showed him his and said, "Mine is more important then yours." He then turned to the shore patrol and said, "If this man is not off the property in ten seconds shoot him." It did not take the aide ten seconds to clear the property. The guard said, "Oh shit, admiral, I would have liked to put a shot right in his ass." Adam said, "Son, I know just how you feel."

Adam asked Bill if he had any idea how much heroin he collected so far? Bill said, "It looks like twenty tons or more and it is way over what we estimated. We ran out of containers and we're starting to pile the stuff on the floor. These plastic bags of dope tear easy so we have to have something to put this stuff in or we will have it all over the floor."

Adam asked Brad if he had some place to store the dope until they were ready to transport it. Brad said, "We have plenty of space over in the magazine over at North Island."

"Fine" said Adam, "We will guard it here until we move it in the morning." "Brad called and said he located cardboard boxes that will hold sixty pounds apiece and can be stacked six high - much better than bags."

That night Adam put all the truckers up for the night and fed them for all the trouble they went though. Adam told them to eat all the steaks they wanted but no alcohol and no phone calls until they are back in their trucks. Once the drugs moved to North Island, the trucks could be loaded with rice and be on their way. The port captain and Markos never got the phone call. They expected a call and it was driving them crazy. Surely they must have found the heroin by now.

Adam got a call from Dixie and she told them to get down to the dock right away that is all she had time to say. Adam got hold of Bill and took off for the docks. When they got there, they could see over by the other shore that the Pagan Island was down by the bow. The coast guard was there and Adam called Wilson over at the yard and said, "We need pumps and men to shut off the sea valves on the Pagan Island over near North Island.

We need them now before the tide changes and we lose the ship."

The coast guard said the crew opened up the valves to sink the ship and took all the ship's papers with them. They made one mistake when they only put out one bow anchor so the ship turned on the outgoing tide. The ship turned around and the stern was fast on a sand bar. The stern that has most of the important parts like the engines and boilers was high and dry. After four hours of pumping with huge machines on barges, they had it up and floating. They set three more anchors to keep it in deep water.

While all of this was taking place Adam called Gulfport, talked to Cal Williams, and said, "Yesterday when I talked to you it seemed like you were down in the mouth. First let's call each other by our first names; it saves a lot of time. Washington has done it again. They gave me plans that will not fit that piece of rust they also send me". Adam said, "Keep on building that furnace and I will send you a great ship to put it on, like the one I told you about. It will be five hundred and twenty feet long and about eighty some feet wide. It will do some twenty-five knots without a strain". When Adam hung up, he looked across the harbor and saw the Pagan Island up and riding on four anchors. The agent for the ship had called and told Adam that the last owners of the ship were some far eastern outfit that could not be located as many outfits buy a ship or plane, use it for a drug run, then destroy it. Adam thanked the agent and said that was what he needed to know.

Adam called Hal Ladan over at coast guard and asked him for information on the Pagan Island. "That is right. The ship we pumped out yesterday did not seem to have any papers aboard," Hal said. "I figured you would ask for some help so I started a search and here is what I found out. It was built in Sweden, the agent was the Garret Corporation flagged out of Panama and leased to the World Hunger Organization for carting rice. The company that built it went belly-up and later sold it to a company that does not exist any longer. It is the same old story - use it a few times and ditch it. As far as I can see that is why they sank it as then the vessel becomes a salvageable property and if you can attach a line to it, you own it. That is only my opinion."

Adam called his chief petty officer over at North Island and told him to get in touch with Cal Williams down in Gulfport, Mississippi. Have him call me over at the Hilton."

Adam turned to a group in his office and said, "There is an outfit down in Mississippi that is building a furnace to burn hazardous material. The ship Washington sent him is much too small and way too slow. What do you all think we should do with the Pagan Island? I was told that once they sink it whoever grabs it owns it." "Well, we grabbed it."

The phone rang and Adam picked it up. "Hello Cal, remember I said I might have some good news for you. How would you like to have a ship five hundred and twenty feet with a beam of one hundred and eighty feet, diesel-powered, that can do better than twenty-eight knots easy? There are cranes forward and amidships and only seven years old."

"You like? Cost? Oh about ten steak dinners. You will have to burn some narcotics later on for us." Cal said, "You get me that ship and I will even burn a few bodies for you."

"Cal, that will not be necessary just yet." said Adam.

Hal Ladan entered the suite at the Hilton, whistled, and said, "Boy, you navy boys really know how to live. "Adam said, "Hang around; we are going to have steaks for dinner. Hal, I want that ship. I talked to a man in Gulfport, Mississippi and he is building a furnace that goes out on a ship and burns hazardous material. Washington sent him a vessel that is too small and too slow to do the job. Now if we fix up the Pagan Island it will be just right."

Hal said, "You want to steal a ship?" Adam said, "It doesn't belong to anyone and the president said we could have anything we want short of murder. Look, it does not belong to anyone, why not fix it up and put it into the reserve fleet. It is not stealing it, and we are recycling it. Anyone see an objection?" "Hell no, you are an admiral, we all love the idea." Hal said as he looked at the others.

Adam turned to Bill and said, "Get my buddy over at the yard and tell him we need a few things." Bill handed the phone to Adam. "Hello commander, how are you today?"

"What can I get you today?" was his question. Adam said, "Well as long as you ask and I have you on the line. I need a few things. Got a pencil?" "I need some pipe fitters, boilermakers, electricians, welders, and carpenter mates, plenty of steel plate, pipe, and wire. I need a lieutenant that knows his way around a ship, no damned pencil pusher. Oh, and a chief Bo'sun mate and enough ratings to man a ship like the Pagan Island to sail from San Diego to Gulfport, Mississippi. Fill the galley with good food and water, fill up the fuel tanks and yes, plenty of navy grey paint, fix-up papers, and a number for an auxiliary reserve ship."

"Thanks, I am counting on you and your name will be on the promotion list when it is made up." Collins turned to his staff and said" lets eat, I like being an admiral with a big budget"

At dinner Hal said, "Admiral, you remind me of a boy that coaxed a dog to follow him home and then asked his mother if he could keep him." Adam said, "I guess we all did that at one time or another when we were growing up."

Adam turned to Roger Ralston and said, "I need some work from you - first a name and a number for this new reserve ship. Just get me a number for I have a name. Back when they were building the Panama Canal a ship was loading dynamite just outside of Baltimore,

Maryland harbor when it caught fire because a loader used a baling hook which was against the rules and the ship blew up. Only one man lived, he was on a tug that went back to pick men out of the water. This man lived because in those days the tugs were fired by coal and he was down in the boiler room at the time. The tugboat blew off around him. I went to school with his grandson. That is a part of history that people forget"

The number for the newly invented ship is E.P.A. 100. That is for the environmental protection agency as they will take procession once it is put in regular service after the shakedown and training.

Dinner was over and they retired to their rooms, Roger said, "I could spend the rest of my tour of duty living like this." Hal said, "Nah, too soft." And they went down the hall to their rooms laughing.

Adam turned to Bill and asked, "Would you like to take a flight out of North Island tomorrow?" That was like asking a child if it would like some candy. Adam did not wait for an answer. "Okay, 0800 and pack suntans and a set of blues; we may be gone for a spell."

A twin-engine jet was waiting for them when Story showed up; he greeted Adam who said that he was waiting for one other person. A car pulled up and out stepped a good-looking female Lt   Commander, wearing navy wings of gold. She got her bags and turned around; Bill was shocked when he saw who it was. Adam said, "Let me introduce you to Lt. Commander Helen Able." Bill said,

"Are you able?" to which she replied, "You bet your ass I am sailor." Bill's face got red as always and he said, "First, you are Dixie North then you are Sara West and now you tell me you are Helen Able - just who the hell are you?" She replied, "You will find out someday, sailor."

Adam said, "Stop the small talk, get on the plane," Bill said. "Adam, that is no way for a Lt Commander to talk to a Captain in the U.S. Navy. I could haul her in for captain's mast".

Adam said, "We are wasting time. Get in the left seat and get ready to take off." Helen got in the co-pilot's seat and off they went. Adam told Story to head 98 degrees and he would explain later. "Meanwhile, let the commander take the controls." Bill asked, "Can she fly this plane? It is fast." Adam said, "She may fly circles around you some day soon."

As they were crossing over the Mississippi River, Adam said, "Head for the air station at Jacksonville, Florida. I think you have flown out of there a few times. This is going to be our base of operations for awhile." Adam moved into the pilot's seat and got on the radio when they were a half hour out. He called Jax.and asked to be patched through to Captain Anton. "This is Admiral Collins." In a minute Joe Anton was on the horn "Hi Adam, nice to hear from you again, I have been expecting you. Brad and a company of marines landed here two hours ago and wouldn't let anyone near their plane. What are you carrying - gold?"

Adam said, "Much more valuable than that." Joe said, "I never saw so many marines guard one plane in my life."

Adam asked Joe to set up a private room for lunch and he would explain everything over one of their famous steaks. "We will need two cars when we land." "No problem." was the reply.

Adam introduced Joe to Helen at the officers club and to Bill's surprise Helen hugged Joe and kissed him on the cheek. Bill said, "She can't keep her hands off handsome sailors - do you two know one another?" Joe's face turned red and said, "She flew out of here many times and flew with me out of Millington, Tennessee, before budget cuts broke up a great squadron. In order to stay in she had to transfer to another branch - she chose Naval Intelligence." "Too bad, she was becoming a damned good pilot."

Adam said, "Let's eat and I will tell you what this is all about. Most of the group is already here. I will refresh your memories by introducing you all again. First, we have Joe Anton, the commanding officer of this air station; Harry Carter his exec.; George Beck, customs; Hal Ladan, coast guard; Roger Ralston, naval intelligence; Henry Green, A.F.T.; Mark Kent border patrol; Will Milford, army; Woody Miner, California state police; and Brad Wilson marines. They are the ones guarding the plane. The heavily guarded plane is carrying enough pure heroin to pay all of our salaries for the next hundred years. It is worth billions, that's right that is spelled with a 'B' and it will be stored here in a magazine and added to over the next several weeks with other narcotics that will be collected throughout the country. The folks here at Jax, are going to be busy seeing that all types of aircraft are landed here safely. Joe will be very busy giving out call letters of identification to his people in the towers."

Adam said to Bill and Helen, "Get yourselves unpacked, check out a car, and see the sights. Jacksonville Beach is one of the finest around. Drive over to St. Augustine and see Fort Marco and the Fountain of youth. Oh, and when you go there bring me back a few cups of it, there are some days I could use some." "I have a meeting with Naval Intelligence; I will see you both at breakfast."

Bill and Helen toured St. Augustine and nearby areas then stopped for dinner in South Jacksonville at a little seafood restaurant built out over the St. Johns River. As they ate a great seafood meal Bill looked at Helen and realized he was starting to have feelings for her. She was smart, had a great sense of humor, was very pretty, and had a body of a twenty year old. He began to wonder how old she was but he sure was not going to ask, that is for sure. Returning to the base Bill took a shower and sat back to watch television when there was a knock at the door. He slipped on a robe and answered it. There was Helen with a shaker of whiskey sours and two glasses that she sat down on a small table. Bill was surprised, but should not have been for this woman is used to getting her own way. While Bill stood there with his mouth wide open, Helen said, "Close the door and your mouth and pour the drinks."

Bill pulled his robe closed; Helen let hers fall open, and after a few drinks neither had robes on. They headed for the bedroom. Bill had only bedded one woman in his whole life and was not sure how he would perform. Helen reacted to his slow moves then showed him some positions he never dreamed of. They woke at 0800 and Helen said she had to go across the hall to her room to mess up the bedclothes to make it look like she slept there last night. At breakfast Adam was waiting for them, He noticed they were smiling and he was pleased.

Adam said, "There is a plant in town that produces farm chemicals and mixes products for other companies. Naval Intelligences tells me they are in financial straits and I think I can do business with them. The company's name is the Jacobs Brothers. Two brothers own it and they are about as different as cats and dogs. One is the office manager, his name is Cody, and the other runs the plant, a real bum - heavy drinker and gambles more money them he makes, his name is Glen. His wife found out he was on dope and screwing around and that was the straw that broke the camel's back. She left him and said she would take him to court and take anything he had left."

Cody Jacobs came back from vacation to find his brother had fired the bookkeeper and had withdrawn a hundred thousand from the company reserve fund that was set aside for a new mixer that was currently sitting in a warehouse across town just waiting for the concrete footings to cure before installing the new machine. The word got out on Glen's problem so they will deliver only on C.O.D.

Cody asked Glen where the money had gone. Cody said, "I had to pay off some people or they would hurt me real bad, after all half the money in this business is mine anyhow. If we need money, why don't we do as we always do, take out a loan?" Cody said that their credit was so bad that no one will touch them now. "The mixer is sitting in a warehouse and we cannot install it without money."

Adam made an appointment to see the brothers and showed up as they were going at each other pretty heavy. He introduced himself as Bruce Adams, broker for a large corporation who may do some business with them. Cody said that this not a good time to talk but Bruce offered that he may be able to help them if they agreed with his terms. "I may be able to get you the money to buy those new machines sitting across town and have them installed next week."

Bruce said, "I could get this company out of the hole if you do as I say. First, take the money that you have left and move it into an account that only Cody and a trustee from the bank can withdraw. I can get enough money to pay off the difference and a bonus on top of that. Here is my card. Call me by nine a.m. in the morning or I will take my business elsewhere."

Adam went over to the firm that was sitting on the machines that they had built for the Jacobs Brothers and struck up a deal. Since this type of mixer and silo combination was custom made, they were pretty much stuck with it. The Sable Company that built this machine was glad to see anyone that would make them an offer to take it off their hands. Adam made them an offer at a price that was half the price that the Jacobs Brothers were going to pay for it. In addition, that included installation.

Early the next day Bruce Adams got a call from Cody Jacobs agreeing to his proposal. They figured they had everything to gain and nothing to lose. "Fine, "said" Bruce, "can you meet me at the manufacturer's warehouse this afternoon about two and bring a check for half of the cost of the equipment signed by you and a representative of the bank? Make the check out to The Sable Company." "This works out that Adam gets the equipment for nothing. The agreement was for getting complete control over the mixing and packaging until he is finished using it for his project. The equipment will be sealed off and not be used until he says so.

When Adam got back to the base he made a call over to a part of the Cecil Field complex. He wanted to be connected to a small part of the base called Yellow Water and it was over on the other side of the state hi-way; an old part that was used for a gunnery school back in world war two and the home of Admiral Dale Owings. Admiral Collins wanted very much to meet the man that was a legend; people had said this man knows everything.

Adam made an appointment to meet Admiral Owings at 0800 the next day. The admiral told Adam to come for breakfast and bring a few changes of clothing. Adam told Bill and Helen that he would be gone for a few days, in addition, asked them to help Brad and his marines put the drugs that were arriving every day from all fifty states into the bins according to their type. This was important for the way they will be treated.

Adam got a car, driven by a marine, over to Yellow Water which is about a forty-five minute trip from the Jax Air Base. At the gate of Yellow Water, they were stopped and Adam, after identifying himself, was transferred to another car driven by a marine stationed there at Yellow Water. The marine that brought him there was sent back to base. The front gate called ahead and when Adam got to the admiral's quarters, he was met by the admiral himself as he got out of the car. Owings shook Adam's hand and had all Adam's gear taken upstairs to his room. They had a great breakfast and after coffee got to know each other a bit.

Admiral Owings turned out to be a very complex person. He had joined the navy when he was but sixteen by lying about his age. He took advantage of every opportunity. First, he went to pharmacy school; next to Chemical Engineering College; then on to a college term on logistics. He knew how to make it, how it could be used, how to store it, and how to transport it safely. All this and yet he envied Adam for being where the action was. "I would trade with you anytime. Here I am blowing my own horn when I should be a better host." "What brings you to my part of the world?"

"Admiral Owings, I have a problem that I hope you can help me with," answered Adam. Owings said, "The first problem we have is to stop calling each other 'admiral'; let us get it down to 'Adam and Dale' as I do not care for formalities anyhow."

"Dale, the president has given me a job to do that has never been handled successfully. Everybody that had this job was afraid of treading on somebody's toes." "Dale, I do not give a shit whose toes I injure, I just want to get the job done. The president has given me permission to do pretty much what I want to do to get the job done, period."

Owings told Adam that he liked him and he will do what ever needed to be done to help him. "I read all the letters that come out so I know you need plenty of help - where do we start?"

"Dale, I am sitting on about thirty tons of narcotics most of it pure heroin that we took off a ship from the Far East. What I need is some kind of chemical to mix with it so consequently, when it is used will make people very sick, very fast, and last about a week. I want them so sick that they want to die, but I do not want to kill anyone."

Dale answered, "That does not sound too complicated, just get me some samples of your product and we will run some tests tomorrow. Meanwhile, tell me how far you have come with your organization."

Adam said, "In the months I have had this job some call it the drug czar. The president gave me this position because no one else has the guts to do it properly." "I am going to retire shortly and I don't need the money. I am fed up with the politics and I don't need to make new friends. So what do I have to lose?" "I have a board of directors that comes with all sorts of military and civilian expertise. We go after the drug community like no other law enforcement agency. We push the envelope right into their backyard. Maybe it is not always legal but we get results." "Washington is upset and we are ready to fight so as long as we have the president on our side we will do a good job."

Adam continued, "I am getting off the subject – sorry." "This is our plan: we have collected over thirty five tons of heroin and other types of narcotics that are not to be destroyed but will be mixed with a substance and put out on the street."

"Dale, This where your knowledge comes in," said Adam. "With your permission, I will call over to my office at J.A.X. to have them send over whatever amount of drugs you need."

"If you have different types send me a little of each, label them and since the largest amount is heroin send me a larger amount of it," Dale instructed, "as we may need a different formula."

Adam called over to Brad and asked him to sent six ounces of heroin and smaller samples of each of the other drugs. "Be sure to label them and send them over with two armed marines right away." "Do you have anyone there to help you?"

Brad said, "Harry Carter is here - he will do fine."

After another drink, Dale showed Adam his lab that was as modern as any in the world. "Here I can do things others only think about. I have mice, birds, and guinea pigs. You name it, I have it." "There is a chemical I have in mind; we used it to debug planes that came back from the jungles. It worked great until we found out it made our men sick and had to be discontinued. I have a lot of it because as I said I don't throw anything away, I just have it sent here."

Dale called the main gate and asked an aide to bring five pounds of the chemical from the blue drums in building eleven. In five minutes he had it.

The marines that brought the drugs from the air station were being held up at the main gate. It seemed that they didn't want to give up their goods and the Yellow Water guards wouldn't let them pass.

Adam called, talked to the marines and told them it was okay to give the gate marines their package and thanked them for not wanting to give it up without permission. Adam asked, "Do you trust your people?"

Dale answered, "With my life!" "Let me tell you about these marines." "All of them have seen heavy combat; many have had serious wounds that would have required their separation from the corps so I got them transferred here to serve out their time until they can retire. They are on three and off two. They eat what I eat and every last one of them would take a bullet for me. I take care of them and they take care of me and my base. There is nothing that moves or goes on at this base they don't know about. You may have noticed that the man who took your bags and served you dinner only has one hand. What would he be doing if they let him go? He would probably be a drunk and be found dead in an alley. He has eight years to go before a pretty good pension. Not only that, we have a savings plan at a local bank and some of these guy are worth a pretty good sum."

Dale made a call and in minute there was a car and driver at the door. "Let's take a ride around my base." "This is a carryover from an old gunnery school that had three magazines and now we have over a hundred. We have the most powerful and modern weapons in the world, before you ask, the answer is yes, we have them!!"

When they returned to his house Dale thanked the young driver and called him by name, "You see I treat my men as equals, not military, and it works."

After dinner, they sat around and shot the breeze about the good and bad bases they had served on over the years. After Adam retired Dale went out to his lab and mixed up some formulas he wanted to try on mice so he could see the results in the morning. He mixed the heroin with one strength and the street drugs with a diluted one that was less potent.

The next morning Dale said that he had some time so he could show Adam around the place. The first floor was the admiral's quarters, the great room, the dinning room and poolroom. The second floor had four bedrooms, each with bathroom. Adam said, "I have been all over the world and have never seen anything as lavish - even the navy's largest ships never had anything like this." They sat out on the porch and Dale said, "Not everything we have here is weapons or ammunition. I have material that the higher-ups think was buried or thrown over board." "Like I said, I never got rid of a thing that I might need someday. If they need something and ask me, nice, I will get it for them. If they come looking for something without asking, they would not find it. I have an inventory system code they cannot break. That is why I am still here. I am like J. Edgar Hoover, way past retirement age, but they are afraid to push me for I know where all the bodies are buried."

They went out into the lab and found two mice dead and two who could hardly stand up because they were so sick. The admiral gave two more mice a much lighter dose and to see if they would live through the night.

"Dinner will be seafood and steak. Is there anyone you would like to come and join us?"

Adam said, "Why yes, I have two of my finest, a captain and an. Lt. Commander." "Fine," said Dale, "Call them and see if they can join us at 1900. Tell them to bring extra uniforms and stay the night; I love company."

Adam called to invite them and told them it was a little over a thirty minute drive. "Leave your car at the gate and someone will bring you to the admiral's quarters."

At 1845 they switched cars at the main gate and were met at the driveway by Dale and Adam. "Well," said Dale, "I did not expect someone as pretty as this young woman as my guest." Introductions were made and they all sat down for dinner. Adam said, "This is with out a doubt the best meal you will ever get on any service base, equal to the best restaurant anywhere."

They had no idea anyone in the service ate that well. After coffee, the stories got around to the good old days so Bill and Helen excused themselves and went up to their rooms.

In a short time, Helen showed up with a pitcher of apricot sours. It seems that she can get more with her looks and a few dollars than any one person that Bill knew. They had their drinks and watched television before retiring. In the morning, Helen had to race across the hall to make her room look like she had slept there.

Dale said to Adam, "Do you thing they are sleeping together?"

"I sure hope so, if they are not, Bill is a big fool and I do not think of him as a fool," said Adam.

After they ate breakfast, Dale led them to his lab. There they found two more mice that could hardly stand up. Dale said, "The other night I heard you order six ounces of pure heroin, but when I weighed it before I used any, there were only four ounces. All of the cut drugs were there so maybe it was some sort of mistake. No matter, we had plenty to run the test."

"Here are the percentages to use with the different types of drugs. I will send you a few drums of the chemical I used and it will be labeled DiMethyl Phosphate. Here's a small sample; it is more crystal then a powder. You will have the drums delivered to you sometime in the morning.

When they all got back to J.A.X. Adam called Brad and asked him to meet him over at the magazine. When they met, Adam asked, "Brad," "Exactly what did you send when I asked you for six ounces of the pure grade heroin?"

Brad said, "I weighed each bag and there were six one-ounce plastic bags of heroin." "I put them in a box with the other narcotics, sealed it up, and gave it to the waiting marines."

Adam told him to go through the exact moves he made. Brad said, "I got the bags together and needed scotch tape to seal the box. I went to the next desk to get some and when I got back Harry had the box closed and was waiting for me to seal it." "Is there something wrong?"

Adam said, "I do not know yet but we will soon find out - keep this all to yourself."

The drums of Dimethyl phosphate were received at the Jacobs' plant where the new machinery was being installed. The place would be kept under constant guard until the current operation was over. Adam, Bill, and Helen flew back to San Diego for a board meeting the next day. The board was called to order and each member reported their activities since the last meeting. Most of the action was taking place along the Mexican Border. Mark Kent said they were inspecting trucks that were coming north and finding large amounts of cocaine. Customs officer George Beck said they were inspecting containers at a higher percentage due to the extra help from the army. A.F.T. Henry Green said that the added pressure on the street is removing many vendors and they were picking up large amounts of all kinds of narcotics. Woody Miner of the California State Police reported that all fifty states were collecting drugs along the interstate hi-ways and great amounts at the toll plazas up and down the Atlantic routes, notably Route Ninety-five. He said that ship captains, under the threat of losing their licenses, were turning in smugglers who were using their ships. These officers make a great annual salary and if they lose the right to sail in U.S. waters, they figure the little amount the smugglers pay to ship on their ships, it really is not worth it.

Adam Collins told the board, "All drugs collected should be flown to the Naval Air Station at Jacksonville, Florida, as soon as possible. All costs will be paid out of the drug enforcement budget. You are all doing a great job and it is showing up on the cities' streets. The formulas are being worked out and we should be ready for operation in two or three weeks." "The next meeting will take place in four weeks - possibly in Jacksonville." "Meeting adjourned."

Adam took Brad over to the side and told him to keep all drugs separate until they are classified because they do not work as well if they are all mixed. Adam caught Roger's eye and beckoned him over to hear what he had to say to Brad. He said, "There are two ounces of pure heroin missing. Brad weighed out six packs of one ounce each and when he went to the next desk to get some scotch tape two ounces got side tracked." "I want naval intelligence to get on this very quietly and find it before it leaves the base. Harry Carter was the only other one around so we will start with him. I make it a point to trust everyone I work with so let us go to work on this." "Rodger, all communication on this problem goes through me. No written notes, phone calls and e-mails go through me, understood?" "Absolutely no leaks, period. Use only your best people." "If any smell of this gets out we will have to answer to the press on every move we make." "I have sent Harry and Peggy up to Chicago the find out why their reports are slow coming in; this gives us a chance to search their house."

Meanwhile, over at the rear of the huge Jacksonville Air Base, Harry and Peggy's daughter, Megan, was driving to work through the area where the new buildings were being constructed. The roads were made of material dredged from both sides of the road to make it above the marsh so it could be used to drive on. She came around a curve too fast to see a truck stopped in the middle of the road. She swerved too late and her car turned over in a ditch. The newly filled gas tank split open and caught fire. The men working out of the truck tried to get to her, but they were too late. The fire department was at another part of the base hosing down a plane that had come in on its belly.

As soon as Adam heard about the accident, he sent word for Harry and Peggy to return to the base. The Chaplin met them and they all went into a private room where the tragic events were explained to them. Harry said that their daughter had problems but she was working them out. Her pay just about paid for her rent, auto, and food. An autopsy was out of the question; there was almost nothing to bury. The tags on the car were the only means of identifying the remains.

Adam said to Brad, "Let's go over everything that took place the night of the missing drugs." They all went out to the magazine again and Brad went through the whole movement again. "I weighed out six one-ounce plastic bags of heroin: put them with the others in a box that Harry held until I got the tape. Harry wrapped the box and I put it into a secure bag then handed it a marine to be taken over to Yellow Water." Adam looked around and spotted two plastic bags on the floor. "What are these?" as he picked them up carefully so as to not smudge any prints.

Brad looked down in disbelief as Adam picked up two plastic bags just like the ones he had put an ounce of heroin in. They weighed exactly one ounce each. Brad's face turned red and he said, "They were not here the last time we were here." "Yesterday, I was here with my top sergeant and we went over everything just like we did when we first heard that two ounces were missing." "I can call him as my witness if you like."

Adam likes to over talk things over food so they went to lunch. Adam said, "We can figure this out if we look at all angles; only two people had keys to the magazine - Brad and Harry." "Brad was with us or his sergeant all the time so let's take him off the list. That only leaves Harry, but how and when?"

Brad said, "No vehicles passed the checkpoint, except us, in the last three days. Harry does not look like the type that would walk five miles in and five miles back in all this swamp and thick woods.

Adam said, "Do not sell Harry short; he walked out of the jungle almost thirty miles after his plane went down. He never gained back the lost weight that he lost.

Let's assume this is the way it happened until I dig into this a little farther."

The next morning Adam called Bill into his Quarters. "Bill, this is what I believe happened to the two ounces of heroin that was missing and then mysteriously showed up. I want you to take Harry Carter aside and, off the record, sit down and have a talk, sort of man-to-man.

Bill called Harry and told him he wanted to have a business lunch with him. They had lunch and then Harry asked Bill, "What is this business you wanted to talk to me about? I know I didn't get to Chicago to do what I was sent to do but I got the information over the phone and ran it through my computer. The report is on the admiral's desk."

"Harry, two ounces of pure grade heroin was missing and Brad and you held the only two keys to the magazine.

Harry said, "You all got your heads together and are saying that I stole two ounces of heroin, is that it?"

Bill answered, "Harry, I am here to do you the biggest favor of your career and if you listen I may be able to save your ass." "What you say to me today could not only save your retirement, but also keep you out of jail, are you reading me?" "Tell me, what was the deal with the heroin?"

"Bill, I did not know where to turn and here is the truth. My daughter is an addict and has been for over ten years. My wife and I have spent more money then we had to send her to clinics all over the world. I thought that if we got her a job here and lived close we could finally get her to straighten out." "Last week I found she was back on dope big time; she maxed out her credit cards and said she was not going to any more farms to get off drugs."

Harry continued, "I saw the opportunity to get my hands on some pure heroin and I took it. I put it in my bathroom hoping she would find it and use it. Being pure, it would kill her. Anyone that has been through what Peggy and I have been through over the years may think the same as I did." "I realized that assisting my daughter to kill herself was a big mistake but I was to a point that I could not think straight any longer. I returned the heroin to the magazine where it would be found as if it had fallen by accident when Brad and I were packaging it. I went through the swamp and woods at night to put it back."

"Bill, nothing they do to me could be any worse than what we have gone through for the last ten years. Do what you have to do, please, and get it over with."

Harry said, "My only child died. Peggy and I never shed a tear and for that we are sorry. Peggy is the one that will suffer the most. Our daughter is dead, and with me in jail there will be no pension money coming in. We have no relatives to help and with all she has been through, I do not think she could take it. There is no money at all and she is too old to get a decent-paying job."

That afternoon Bill met with Adam and Roger over lunch and the one thing they agreed on was that they think better over a full stomach. Bill told them all the information he had obtained from Harry and asked them for a fair decision. With this done, he turned and left.

"Okay," said Adam, "Let's look at what we know." "Was anything stolen?" "NO." "Did we need those two bags to complete our test?" "NO." "How many of us could go through what Harry and Peggy did without breaking?" "NONE." "Did any information about this incident get out?" "Good God, I hope not." "What we have here is compassion for a fellow officer who has gone through hell over the last ten years. We may not know the complete story but we have to decide on a sentence."

They all voted to have Harry retire and not speak of this matter under threat of punishment. Under the terms of their agreement, Harry would have no knowledge of who came down with this decision. Should he choose not to agree with the decision, he would stand on article thirty-four and a general court martial.

Bill met with Carter and laid down the rules. Harry almost collapsed when he heard the offer and he added that Peggy had had no knowledge of any of his actions. Harry then said, "I will turn my request for retirement in today. I was too ashamed to tell Peggy but she will be glad to move to some place and settle down as we have been moving for most of our lives."

"Thank you for all your efforts on my behalf, Bill, you really saved our lives."

On the way to Gulfport, Mississippi, the newly named Allan Chime was completely done over. The wheelhouse was moved forward, the crews' quarters were moved under the wheelhouse, far enough away from any fumes that the new furnace may put out. Everything had a fresh coat of navy grey paint. The crew had most of the heavy work done before they reached the canal. They liked taking a rest and acting like tourists as they traveled through the Panama Canal. All was ready for the big furnace when they arrived at the yard at Gulfport.

Cal Williams was glad to see a ship of this size and knew it was perfect for the furnace that he designed and built from scratch. After the ship tied up, Cal threw the crew a party like they have never seen before - more seafood, steaks and drinks than they could handle. They were treated like royalty during the week of liberty before heading back to San Diego. Back on the west coast, Adam got a call from Cal; the Allan Chime was the right size with twin engines that would more then do the job. He also told Adam that the crew had done a great job modifying the old Pagan should be done within three or four weeks and I would love to show you the ship when the work has been completed."

The navy crew consisted of first class mechanics and they enjoyed the week liberty they had here. "We sent them home smiling." Cal said, "You said you were renaming the ship and putting it in the reserve fleet because that way the government will pick up the bill of coming through the canal." "It serves them right for sending me that piece of junk to work with." "We now have plenty of living room and space for anything you will have to burn." Adam replied, "Thanks; we will see you soon and take you up on that offer of steaks."

Over at the mixing plant in Jacksonville, Glen Jacobs reported that the plant would be operational in two weeks and that he needed a two-ounce sample of heroin in order to calibrate the screens. Brad was again asked for two ounces of heroin and he reluctantly sent the samples over to the plant under marine guard.

Brad had all different types of drugs in different colored plastic bags. Planes were coming in from all over the country just as Adam said they would. This kept the tower busy dealing with all kinds of people unfamiliar with the system they operate under. Adam told Joe to stick with it, for most of it will be over in two weeks.

Bill and Helen flew back to JAX to inspect the mixing plant before it went into operation and here they found everything brand new. They were amazed at all the stainless steel - the mixer, the silos, and all the connecting pipes. Glen Jacobs showed them around and explained the operation. "Here is where we start by pouring the main product in here and the secondary product in the hopper on the right. Be very careful not to drop any plastic in either hopper for that will require a shut down that will take hours to untangle." Please be careful and explain to anyone that works this part of the operation to do the same." Bill said that he, alone, would be on this part of the job. Glen went on to tell Bill, "The mixer runs much faster then the packager so after the mix everything goes up to the silo on the third floor and the next day it is brought down as is it needed. This will work until the silo is empty. Also, on the side of the packager a sample will come down every tenth pallet load so that you do not have to open any of the bags to get a sample - just use the contents of the sample tube."

After Glen left the plant, he went to his favorite bar and met with his bookie and loan shark. He had a sample of the heroin that he showed his bookie and said, "I can get enough of this to make us even and give me a million on the side." Margo the bookie gave Glen a couple of grand and told him, "If this does not work out your ass is mine!"

Adams was hoping that by giving Glen a sample of the good stuff the gang would find a way to hi-jack it after it leaves the plant. It looked like the plan was working. Adam had two men in the bar when Glen came in to meet Margo at a rear table and they took pictures of the meet.

At the board meeting, Adam reported that the plan was coming together nicely. The amount of the drug to mix was more than they expected, for what was picked up on the street just poured in. The drugs that were picked up at the border by the A.F.T. people did a great job on the streets. The border patrol, by opening containers, found huge amounts trying to be smuggled in. The state police of all the states were surprised at what was being picked up on the interstates. The plan that was spread around was that all these drugs were going to be taken to Gulfport, Mississippi, to be put on a ship then taken out to sea to be burned. Adam said, "Isn't it a little ironic that the ship that brought in such quantities of drugs is going to be the ship that takes those same drugs out to burn them?

Adam continued, "Our plans were different than what was spread around. We will mix it all with the chemical agent that was tested over at Yellow Water and expect to have it stolen. Because we have no way to distribute it, the people who steal it will do that job for us." "These people have been moving drugs all over the country for years and they have been very good at it. In order for them to have the time to do their thing this will be a good time to give all your people time off. A week's vacation with pay should to it and tell them it is for doing such a great job."

"We hope that once the people use the mixture we are working on, it will make them so sick they may give up the habit altogether. When we move it from Jacksonville to Gulfport, we expect them to make their move. The trucks will be lightly guarded and will offer no resistance. The word is out that we are going move a large amount of drugs out of Jacksonville and that we're going to stop overnight at a truck stop not to far northwest of Jacksonville. They will be guarded by marines in civilian clothes and unmarked cars; one in the front and one in the rear. They will be in touch by phone to the trucks." "They are there just to keep an eye on things."

Adam asked if there were any questions. "This is a new type of operation and if anyone has some suggestions, let us hear them.....none?" "Okay, the meeting is adjourned."

Woody Miner took Adam aside and asked, "What, if any, side effects will there be to this mix once it gets out on the street?" Adam said, "This is completely new and we are not all sure. I know that there will be questions coming in from the other forty-nine states so let us wait and see. I will keep you informed as we go along."

"Starting a week and a half we will give our people a week off; this will give the drug organization time to distribute our product all over the country. This is what we need to make our plan work."

Adam told Bad Wilson and Bill Story; "I want all the drugs over to the mixing plant by 0900 tomorrow. We have to get this operation going." We will have security all around this plant until we are finished with it." "Brad, this no time to have any of our drugs stolen so arm your men and tell them to shoot anyone trying to break in."

Bill said, "Boy!" "That will look good on the front page of all the papers in the country."

Adam said, "When you are trying to do something important, you cannot fart without them asking a lot of questions. The press is a pain in the ass and if something happens I will just have to face up to it."

The next morning trucks were backing up to the building and Bill told them to unload as the bags were needed. All personnel were to remove all rings and any chains so as not to interfere with the operation. They were told to also tape their coveralls at the ankle and wrist. They were to wear facemasks to keep from breathing in any of the powder.

"We do not want anyone getting high before the day is over."

Mixing started with Bill emptying the bags into the mixer - first one bag of drugs to two bags of the powder Admiral Owings send over. Everyone, except Story, took turns for a break to get a drink and something to eat. Bill drank coffee and had a few donuts until the job was finished. All was mixed and sent up to the silo. At 1800, the mixer was shut down and was cleaned first by rotating air jet; what was cleaned was sent up also. Next came the water jets that completed the job. They inspected everything and found out it was clean and shiny.

All were allowed to order from the local pizza and sub shop and charged it all to Adam. The men removed their shoes and coveralls and used air hoses to blow the dust off them. For security, reasons all except the officers would spent the night.

The next morning they got ready to package the mix in ten-pound bags that were piled on pallets with every tenth pallet having a sample of what was in the bags. This took a lot longer than expected for with all the drugs coming in from all over the country they ended up with an added amount. They finished up by 1500 and by putting an equal amount in each truck it took up more time. Finally, the trucks got on the road and about an hour out of Jacksonville a state trooper pulled them over on the shoulder. The marine lieutenant came up from the following car and asked the trooper what was the matter. The police officer said that the trucks did not have a state sticker on their tags allowing them to travel on a state road. He was about to write a ticket when the lieutenant showed his I.D. card and said, "We are hauling government material." The officer said that didn't carry any weight with him. One of the marines that were riding in the following car came forward carrying an AK 47 and asked what the problem was. The officer looked at more guns then he had ever seen. He saw that he was way over his head and apologized for stopping them. The lieutenant told him to turn around and go back the way he came and not to tell anyone he got in the middle of a secret operation. The men at the station house probably would not believe him anyway so the officer did as he was told and the trucks were on their way.

The convoy was late getting to the truck stop because of being stopped on the highway by the state police. They parked backed up to the woods they went in to eat and bunk down for the night as they had two marines working in shifts back in the darkness to keep an eye on the trucks.

The next morning they found the vehicles just where they left them and no sign of them being broken into.

Brad called Adam and told him of the run in with the state trooper and for some reason Adam found it funny. He told Adam that the trucks were as they left them.

Adam said, "Maybe they will make a move on the road and if they don't, park the trucks outside the shipyard gates and leave them unguarded." "Call me in the morning."

They traveled at a slow pace and took a long lunch hour before reaching the shipyard at Gulfport. Wouldn't you know the same state police officer that stopped them the night before pulled up along side and this time he just waved.

They parked the trucks as instructed and reported to Cal Williams. He invited every one to come aboard for some dinner and to spend the night in some nice clean bunks. The next morning the marines said, "No one even came near the trucks during the night." Brad said, "Oh crap!" "Adam is not going to be happy hearing that."

He called and gave him the bad news, he was right Adam was unhappy. Adam said, "Bill, Helen and I will fly out to see you in about four hours. Meanwhile ask Cal how he wants you to unload. Oh, and tell Cal we still we still want that steak dinner for sending him the Allan Chime." "See you for lunch."

Bill and Helen joined Adam on the flight to Pensacola where they picked up a navy car and drove over to Gulfport. At the shipyard office, they met Brad and

Adam. Adam said, "Are these people that stupid?" "They could have had a billon dollars worth of narcotics almost for the asking - where did we go wrong?" "We had this planned out so well."

"Let's go aboard, talk to Cal and see when he will be ready to take our material." Cal met them at the gangplank and invited them all to have lunch. "Why all the long faces?" "I have the steaks as I promised."

They all went aboard the Alan Chime and could not believe it was the same ship. It looked like a completely new one. The wheelhouse was moved forward and under that were the new crews' quarters. This would get them out of the way of any dangerous fumes. All the way aft was the furnace they heard so much about - it was huge, and had the funnels raked back on each side at a fifteen degree angle to better carry away the fumes. "We will move to another pier where the ships cranes can do the work and there are some tank cars there we'll be off loading."

Cal said," Okay, I think it's steak time." The meal was as great as expected; Cal said it was the best beef available. After the meal, the three flew back to Jacksonville and As Cal was seeing them off he turned and said, "Adam, anytime you need me just give me a call. You seem to have more cargo than you planned." Adam answered, "We picked up a lot since I talked to you last, all in all about thirty five tons." Cal asked, "Is it all powder?" Adam said, "Yes, our people all over the country have been working hard to collect that.

"No problem," said Cal, "We have plenty of room."

On the way back To Jacksonville Adam was down in the dumps and asked Bill and Helen, "Where are we going to get enough drugs to put together another plan like that?" Bill said, "Cal will take all our hard work out on a shake-down cruise and burn it up."

Two days later Cal called and asked if he on a secure line. Adam figured it must be important for Cal to ask and he replied, "Yes, it is." Cal said that he was out in the gulf on a shake-down and he found something very strange. He said he checked the bags three times and got the same results. "Adam, what do you want me to do with thirty five tons of weevil infested flour?" "No, there is no mistake."

Adam said, "I checked the samples myself and they all came out perfect." "Adam, I checked them too, and like you said they were correct." "I think you have been taken by the oldest trick in the book - it is called the old switch-a-roo."

Adam asked Cal, "Where are you heading?" Cal said, "Southeast and we will pass Florida on our way out to the Atlantic." Adam asked if it was at all possible to head towards Tampa as he would like to meet him. Cal said, "Sure, we can be there by 1500 tomorrow." Adam told Cal it would take a half an hour for him to fly there in the morning. Cal said, "I will call you to let you know where to be so our captain's gig can pick you up."

Adam told Bill and Helen to be ready the next day by 1300 in order to fly to Tampa to meet Cal Williams.

"Come on in and have a seat." "I just found out why our perfect plan did not work and why no one wanted to hi-jack our trucks - we were not carrying any narcotics." Adam started to laugh as he looked at their faces. They were not sure what he was saying because they followed the mix right from the beginning to the packaging and loading of the trucks.

Bill said, "We checked it al along the way. We checked the samples that were attached to every tenth pallet and everything came out perfect."

Adam said, "We are the victims of a slight of hand and as Owings calls it - the oldest game in the world - the old switch-a-roo. Somewhere there is thirty-five tons of dope going in the direction we wanted it to go without any effort on our part at all." "Cal will explain it all to us tomorrow at 1500. Bring along some old clothes, we may be crawling around on the ship: and also some suntans for we will probably be spending the night."

After lunch, they flew over to Tampa and after talking to Cal, they met the gig at the dock and were taken out to the ship. Cal met them at the gangplank and escorted them down to his office. After being seated, Cal showed them samples of what they thought they had on the trucks and what was really delivered. When laid out side-by-side you could easily see the difference. What they had mixed was a pure white powder with green crystals and what they unloaded on to the ship was brownish white color. The first was taken from the sample pack on every tenth pallet and the brownish powder was the wheat flour packaged in the bags.

"We will burn it and no one will have to know except Admiral Owings and us. The people on the ship do not know what the product is, just that it has to be put in the furnace and destroyed." "Please let's sit on this for a while until we figure how the switch was made and where we expect it to be next week."

They stayed the night and in the morning, called Owings and asked if he would like meet them at the Jacksonville Air Station for lunch. He gladly excepted saying be has not been on the big base in years. At lunch Adam, Bill, and Helen told Owings the whole story as much as they knew up to the present. He laughed and said, "This has happened to me a few times over the years." Owings asked how thought the switch was made and then said to Adam, "Let us wait awhile and see how it all plays out."

The next morning they met and all four sat around the breakfast table. Adam said, "I do not know how they pulled it off. We put the mix in the pans in the percentage you mapped out for us; it got mixed and sent up to the silos on the third floor. The next day it was brought down and packaged and every sample was checked and came out perfect. It was put on the trucks and the trucks were sealed."

Dale said, "They did not have to steal the narcotics from you; they all ready had them. There is an old saying that if you cannot be smart, be lucky."

"I would love to spend the night but the wife of one of my marines is having a baby tomorrow. It is his first and I am to be the godfather. This young man is like a son to me and I cannot disappoint them. These men can go into battle but let their wife have a baby and they all come apart."

They held the board meeting in the Hotel Roosevelt in downtown Jacksonville the next morning because most of the board was on the east coast at the time. Adam said, "It is more crucial then any meeting we have had so far and none of what is said here today leaves this room." "You all know what the plan was that was expected to come off perfectly. Well, I am here to tell you that it came off better than that." "How can it be more than perfect, you ask?" "Well instead of them stealing the narcotics from us on the road, they stole it from us at the mixing plant. We do not know how yet but, we expect it is on its way to points around the country just the way we wanted."

"We do not know yet how they pulled the switch; we had the plant secured right from the start. As it is, they worked our plan better than we could have hoped for. Now that the mixed drug is out on the streets, the next thing we will be looking for is who is calling in sick because they took our drugs and who is showing up at the hospital in pain that is severe that only last for about five days?"

"We do not want our product to be hindered from being spread around but we still want the border patrol and the coast guard to keep doing the great jobs they are doing. We will meet in two weeks in San Diego so please keep your ears open for any news on the streets about how this drug is affecting users. Please write down what you hear and we will digest what we know up to that point." "Meeting adjourned."

The next morning Bill picked up the newspaper and there in big print was the story of the shooting of Glen Jacobs on the parking lot of one of Jacksonville's shadiest nightclubs. Someone put two slugs in the back of his head, execution style. This is the club where Glen met with Margo, his bookie, and loan shark, to make a deal with the sample of heroin that was supplied to him via the plan.

"Helen," "This is your area of expertise." "Call naval intelligence and find out if they can tie us to the crime."

She got on the phone and got things moving. Naval Intell is always busy with all he bases around the Jacksonville area. Adam called police headquarters and made an appointment with the chief of the homicide division. The three of them went in to see Vernon Porter and Adam made the introductions as they were seated. Adam showed his I.D. and told the officer that he was the head of the federal drug task forces. Vernon said that he knew who he was and that he got a copy of the letter that the president sent out. Adam said, "I have to deal with many people and Glen Jacobs was one of them. If my name or organization name comes up in your investigation, I would like you to give me a call. It is a matter of national security."

"Keep this under your hat. We collected thirty-five tons of narcotics and the Jacobs plant did the packaging for us. The dope was sent to Gulfport, Mississippi, and loaded on a ship to be taken out to sea and burned."

Helen told them that Glen Jacobs had some strong connections with some very unsavory people that hung out at the club where he was found dead. He met often with a man named Marty Bankinski also known as Margo. "You may want to talk to him."

The chief said, "Oh yes, we know him; he is a real bad apple." Adam added that if he could be of any assistance please give him a call as he gave Vernon one of his private cards.

They left with a load off their minds and returned to the air station and had dinner. Bill and Helen retired to enjoy each other before the trip back to the west coast in the morning. They thanked Joe Anton for his hospitality and Adam told him there would be more drugs coming in. Brad was going to be here for nearly two weeks and after that someone would come here to take his place. "Any problems, give me a call," said Adam as they left

The next board meeting was held without Helen for she was back at her old job as Dixie collecting information. Adam brought everyone up to speed on how things turned out in their favor in the switching the drugs. "Is there any information coming in on the health reports?" When Adam looked at the reports he saw that people calling in sick had gone up twenty percent, not bad for a start. This figure should change in the next two weeks. Adam said that he would be in Washington on business for a week or so and the next meeting would be in two weeks.

With Adam away and no meeting for two weeks Bill and Helen decided to take some R & R in Cancun. They flew down and checked into a luxurious hotel right on the beach. Since their rooms were on the first floor, they could walk right out on to the white sandy beach. The room had a whirlpool and a bar that was all-inclusive. They unpacked, had some lunch, and put on their suits. This was the first time that Bill really got a full view of Helen as she was putting on her suit. She was five foot ten, about one hundred thirty pounds with beautiful dark hair. All of a sudden, Bill would rather do something other then go swimming. This young woman is like a lovely young model you would find on the cover of a men's magazine.

Helen ran out into the water and called back, "Come on in the water is great." Bill could not run with this swelling in his suit. He managed to get in the water without her noticing his desire. She could swim like a fish, being built with slim waist and broad shoulders. Bill thought he was a good swimmer, but she was swimming circles around him. They lay on the beach for a while until the Mexican sun drove them inside.

They got into the hot tub which was a good way to bring their body temperature down to a comfortable level. They dried each other off while laughing and kissing parts as the towel moved over some of the more sensitive areas. Bill lay down on the king size bed and he pulled Helen on top of him. She expected him to push her down over his nice stiff penis, but instead placed a hand under each cheek of her ass and lifted her until she was sitting over his face. He reached up and separated the lips of her vagina. He licked her swell as he stuck out his tongue and found her swollen clitoris. He licked easy at first and harder as he reached up and rubbed her nipples. She let out a moan as she moved up and down over his tongue. She started to shake and she went off like never before in her life. She moved down Bill licking all the way until she reached his erection, which she took in her mouth and started to suck easy. She added more suction as she moved up and down, she then took his balls gently in her hand. He arched his back and erupted with a sense of great satisfaction.

Helen asked him where he learn that little trick he did on her? He said on long lonely nights on a ship he did a lot of reading. Bill said, "You had a few tricks yourself." Helen replied, "I did a lot of reading too," and with that, they laid back and kissed and had a good laugh. Bill said, "I read about this kind of love, never though I would ever experience any of it." Bill and Helen returned to San

Diego happy but not rested. It was time to go back to work.

Bill called the meeting to order for Adam who was still in Washington. Before Adam went to Washington, he assigned sections of the country to members to watch and report on. He wanted information on those who got sick. He wanted age, sex, body build, and occupation. "Put the word out to all your informants and tell them what we want and call them tonight because we will meet again to morrow."

The next day the board members were ready to report. Bill called the meeting together and said "Before we hear from any of you I would like you to hear from Dixie." She got up and said, "I listen to these truck drivers from all over and they say that there are so many people sick the emergency rooms cannot handle them. They are treating patients out on the steps of the hospital. No one knows what it is although some say it is a type of the flu."

Dixie went back upstairs to go back to work. Woody Miner of the state police said, "You all know that California and the southwest was always the hot bed of the narcotics trade." "No deaths yet but it is early, things are going to get worse. We are having a great number of people just collapsing on the streets. The doctors do not know what it is or how to treat it."

Mark Kent, border patrol, said the south had not had any deaths, but the hospitals are full and the doctors are puzzled. The army has reported that the Chicago area has major problems over what they are calling Asia Green - two deaths so far and many just making it to the hospitals.

Adam called and said that and he and Helen would meet Bill tomorrow in Jacksonville.

When they met the next day Adam said, "Until we get an autopsy we are not certain that any deaths are the fault of our mix." "Just keep you eyes and ears open; we need information." "Use money to talk to cab drivers, door attendants and the local police." "Meeting adjourned."

A call changed their plans. Dixie was to stay in San Diego and Bill would fly to the east coast to meet with Adam. Adam said, "She is more valuable where she is."

After the two met at the air station, Adam said that samples from all over the country were being sent to Yellow Water for Owings to test to see if the diluted mixes were stronger in one area of the country than another. This could possibly give a clue as why more deaths are showing up in one place more than in others. Adam and Bill drove over to Yellow Water and were met with Owings who greeted them. He said, "We have found something interesting."

They went out to his lab where he showed them powder from different parts of the country. The Midwest was cutting their drugs more than other areas. No matter they had the strange properties, they all had amounts of arsenic and worst of all they all have traces of strychnine.

Not enough to kill a healthy person, but could be fatal nonetheless.

"None of that could come from our mix." "I would say it is coming from the cutting rooms but the cut is generally done on the local level. It is cheaper to ship it before it is cut, they do not want to pay to ship milk sugar. The phosphate in my compound could cause the body to absorb the other poisons more readily, even if it was cut down to fifteen percent, this can happen. DiMethyl Phosphate changes once it is in the body for a few hours. This is why it is almost impossible for it to show up in an autopsy."

Owings said, "I think we will find the problem at the mixing plant but I would like to see some of the heroin that you say you kept back at the west coast." Adam said, "The shipyard has a great lab for they test many products that come in from the Pacific so I am sure they will make room for anything you want to do." "Pack up some clothes and we will fly out right after one of your fine breakfasts."

"Adam," "You have yourself a passenger."

On the flight out, they tried to figure out how the dope on the street ended up with arsenic and strychnine in the mix. After they landed, they dressed in civilian clothes and went down to the Moving On restaurant for lunch. Dixie spotted them as they came in the door and with a big smile, she led them to a table. When they sat down Dixie said, "I know you two but who is this handsome stud you have with you?" She thought that she was going to put Owings down but he fooled her and he patted her on the ass. She said, "If you were not so cute, I would slap your face." With that, Adam and Bill almost fell on the floor. Dale said, "What is so funny?" "You two have been laughing ever since we sat down." Adam said that he would explain it later. After the meal, Dixie brought then coffee and said, "Is there anything else, I can get you?" Dale said, "If I were fifty years younger you would not ask that question honey." And again, Adam and Bill almost dropped their coffee.

The lab test over at the shipyard found that the samples were indeed pure heroin which proves that the mix-up was over in Jacksonville. "Okay, tomorrow we go back to the east coast and there we will find the answer." They sat down for dinner at the Hilton and in came Helen in her dress blues and sat down next to Dale. She turned to him and asked, "Hi handsome, see anything you like?" Dale said, "You people set me up at lunch." "They did it to me the first time I saw Helen," said Bill. Dale said, "I meant what I said, if I was fifty years younger." Helen replied, "Maybe I am glad that you are not." This had everybody laughing. Adam turned to Helen, "Pack up and this time we are taking you with us." "Take old clothes because we may be crawling around at the mixing plant.

On the flight back to Jacksonville Helen said to Dale, "I apologize for my actions at the Moving On and then again at the hotel last night." "You were such a sitting duck on both occasions." Owings said, "Honey, you have to be with naval intelligence, no other branch would make you wear such an outrageous outfit like the one you had on in the restaurant yesterday. As for being embarrassed, that doesn't happen to me anymore. It is refreshing to see some humor these days."

After arriving at J.A.X. they all settled down. Adam talked to Cody Jacobs's house keeper who told him that Mr. Jacobs was away for awhile to get over the death of his brother and they should be back on Monday. Checking with naval intelligence Adam learned that trucks took off from the building out back and hit the road heading north. Adam said, "At least they waited until we lifted security before they took off." "They got the stuff out of the plant - but how?"

Adam called Henry Green and asked him to put a watch on a company called World Hunger in Saint Louis. "Don't get too close - we don't want to spook these people until they have distributed all the material they stole from us."

Brad was called and was asked to get together all members of the security force that were on duty at the mixing plant as he would like to talk to them. After rounding them up, Adam asked if anyone had entered the plant while they were doing business. One young marine stood up and said, "Yes sir, one of the Jacobs brothers came back in the evening and said he had to go into the building in the back to turn off the steam and oil the machinery so it would not burn up." "Since it was not the building that we had orders to secure, I figured that it was all right. If I was wrong, it was because I misunderstood the orders."

"Okay, that young man saved our skins." "Make out a report and give it to your commanding officer."

Adam turned to Brad, "Don't make a thing about what this Marine did; I may have done the same thing under the same conditions."

Monday, Adam called Cody Jacobs and asked him to meet them at the plant. At first Cody was reluctant, but relented after Adam said it is very important that they take some samples.

Cody said, "I can meet you at the plant in an hour."

"The material that we brought to your plant was clean but some of it showed up later to have traces of arsenic and strychnine and they must have come from somewhere in the plant." Owings said.

When they met with Cody, Adam said, "Let's go through the whole operation from the beginning."

"We bring our material in and dump it in the trays just like Glen showed us using the percentages that we had figured out. It goes into the mixer it comes out, and went where?"

Cody said, "It then went up to the silos on the third floor." "Fine,"Adam said,"is there any way to get up there from here?" "Yes, and on the way up," Adam said, "I had an understanding that all material we brought here was to go into the new silos."

On the third floor after a short elevator ride, there were pipes running in all directions and they all seemed to go into a large square box. When asked, Cody said that it was called a manifold and connects all the pipes to different silos.

Adam said, "You mean that a mix coming up from the mixer can be put into any of these silos?"

Cody said, "Yes, that is possible but I have not been in this part of the operation for years; my job is sales and management."

Cody gave them small plastic bags to put their samples in. Owings said, "Bill, you and Helen take the even numbered silos and Adam and I will take the odd numbered and the manifold. Use a marker to mark the number on the bags so we can test them later."

It was a good thing that they wore coveralls for this place was nothing but dust. Facemasks were needed for who knows what this dust contains.

On the way out Adam asked Cody, "Is there any way to get from the building out back, I think you call it plant two, into this plant one without going down to the street level?"

Cody said, "Yes, we put a walkway in years ago to save steps going from one building to another."

Owings called Adam, told him that the samples were taken from the mixing plant and told him the story of what took place right from the beginning. Owings said, "Here is what transpired. The samples taken from the new silos contained pure wheat flour give or take a few hundred weevils." "Samples from the manifold were loaded with arsenic and strychnine as well as silos three, four and six." "I have a copy of the orders that were filled prior to our getting involved. The company-filled orders for an insecticide company whose mix contained arsenic and strychnine. Apparently, the silos and the manifold pipes were never cleaned out after their last mixing operation. That answers the first part of our question, the second part is how many will die because of our operation. Were the people that died less than healthy to start with?"

Glen Jacobs came over from plant two that afternoon and switched the manifold to send our products into the silos that were not cleaned out since their last mixing order. Glen was a lot smarter then we figured and a lot more desperate than we thought. He also gave us samples every tenth pallet to give us a sample leading us to think everything was just fine. We were packaging his product as he was packaging ours. All he ended up with was a couple holes in the back of the head face down in a dirty dark parking lot.

Adam told Dale that he had to fly back tomorrow to the west coast for a meeting. "I will keep you informed."

The board was called to order and the representatives gave reports from the different areas of the country. They found that many people were getting very sick and some were dying. The strange thing was they were from all occupations. There were priests, some were police, and even a few were judges. The more education they had the higher the numbers were; maybe that because they could afford to buy the more expensive drugs. The poor were sticking to the practice of smoking marijuana - safer and a lot cheaper.

Autopsies were showing traces of arsenic and strychnine in the bodies, but not in lethal amounts. The pathologists did not have the answers. Collins said we have the tightest of security on this for the press is on everybody's tail to try to make a big story on this without any success. This is driving them crazy. The doctors do not have an answer and we thought that doctors knew it all.

Hal Ladan of the coast guard is doing a great job of finding narcotics in containers and Louis Newman is great tracking ships from ports that are most likely to be exporting drugs to this country. Mark Kent has the Mexican border tightened up. Adam turned to Helen and told her she has to play Dixie for a while longer. "Just keep you ears open and listen to what the dockworkers and truck drivers have to say about the sickness that is going around. They all say that some people are dying and the doctors have no idea why." Henry Green is still trying to break the language these drug people speak; it is a little Spanish, a little pig Latin and even a little Yiddish.

One thing we know and that is this is the way they talked when they were growing up.

President McClour was getting a lot of pressure from the press and since they didn't know that he was not running for a second term, he says, 'the hell with them' "Adam go for broke. That means we pull out all the stops and clean up the drug trade. This is how we go from now on - anything goes." "Meeting adjourned."

Bill brought Laura home from college for the weekend and they were going to the officers' club for dinner and dancing. He said, "Get out your best dress; I want you to look great for I have someone I want you to meet tonight." "She will be meeting us here and I hope you will like her. This could be the one, keep an eye out for her, I have to go to the cleaners to get my dress uniform."

Minutes after Bill left, the doorbell rang. Laura answered and in stepped this big-titted redhead with this big ass. Laura asked if she could help her. "Hi, you must be Laura." "Your dad talks about you all the time. I am his girl friend." "Gee, I have to pee." "That's alright - I know where everything is." And up the stairs she ran.

Bill came in and said, "I see my girl friend's car is out front," "Where is she?" "Is she up stairs getting all prettied up?" Laura started to cry and turned purple with rage, she said, "Daddy how could you?" Bill replied, "What is the matter sweetie; you look like you want to tell me something bad." "Daddy, there is a floozy up stairs, big tits, and big ass and to top it off flaming red hair. Not only has that she said she is your girlfriend." "If she is going to dinner with us I am not going." "Oh!" said Bill, "I see you met the one I expect to marry if she will have me." "Do you think I am good enough for her?"

Just then down the steps comes this beautiful young lady dressed in the uniform of a lieutenant commander wearing her dress white uniform with navy wings of gold. Bill said, "I see you got out of your work clothes and got all cleaned up." Laura did not know what to say.

"My name is Helen and I am with naval intelligence and have to wear some strange clothes sometimes in my job."

Laura said, "Daddy said that you were going to the dance with us and when you showed up dressed like something out of the circus, I thought he had lost his mind."

"I wear that outfit where I work as a waitress." Helen told Laura that she got busy at the Moving On restaurant and did not have time to get out of her outfit

"You see, the people there see me as something like a joke and feel free to talk in front of me. I pick up information that if I dressed neatly they might watch what they say." "I think your father likes the big tits and big ass; he stops in quite often for lunch."

Bill's face had turned blood red by now and Laura told her father to go upstairs and get dressed. "We girls will go out in the kitchen and have a little talk."

After dinner Bill got up to talk to Admiral Collins and this gave Laura a chance to ask Helen if she was going to marry her dad. Helen went over to talk to friend as Bill came back to the table with Adam and Laura asked, "Dad," "Are you going to propose?" Bill said, "I wanted to talk to you first. You know your mother has not been gone too long and I wanted your blessing before I did anything. You know that you are all I have right now."

"Dad, I think she is a great catch and don't let her get away. She will make a cool stepmother and I think mom would approve."

Laura turned to Adam and said, "Dad wants to propose and doesn't know how." Just then, Helen came back to the table and sat down. Adam started to laugh and said, "Bill I have seen you face danger many times but this is the first time I have ever seen you shake all over."

Bill stammered and finally said to Helen, "Would you like to be my bride?" She hugged him and said, "I thought you would never ask." Adam bought champagne and they all toasted the bride to be.

When they got back to the house and were sitting around the kitchen table having coffee Laura dropped a bombshell of her own. She said," I want to go to

Annapolis." "I have given this a lot of thought even before I met Helen, who I may add looks great in that uniform." "College is not doing a thing for me and I feel I am wasting my time."

Bill said, "I will make you a deal - get good grades this year in college and I will do what I can to get you an appointment." "Annapolis is very choosey about students dropping out of school with poor grades and trying to make it in a service academy." "You have some good people pulling for you; a captain for a father, an admiral for a godfather and a step mom who is a lieutenant commander."

Bill and Helen were taking Laura back to college and as they dropped her off, Bill said, "Remember our agreement, good grades or no Annapolis." Laura kissed both of them and said, "You have never seen grades like the ones I will get. Bill turned to Helen," "Laura really likes you and that is important to me. After her mother died, she is what kept me together. She showed me strength I did not know I had. What she thinks means a lot to me."

Helen said," When you proposed to me I wasn't sure you were ready." Bill said, "That night at the officers' club I may not have been, but it was Laura who gave me the shove." "Now she is all excited and told me not to let you get away. She is looking forward to the wedding and is looking for a bride's maid dress."

When they were in bed that night Bill said," I have known you as Dixie North, Sarah West and now Helen Able. Now that we are going to get married maybe, it would be nice if I know your real name. When the pastor says do you take this woman to be your wedded bride, I don't want to ask who?? Not only that, on the wedding invitations we cannot have Bill Story and what's her name invite you to their wedding."

"Hold on to the bed sailor, I do not want you to fall out." "My real name is Stacy Collins."

Bill said, "Good god, have I been screwing the admiral's daughter?"

She replied, "Yes, and with his blessing too."

Bill said, "You mean he has known about us all a long?"

"Sure, that is probably why he had us together so much," answered Stacy.

"I guess Laura knows about all of this too."

Stacy answered, "Oh yes, I told her all about it the other night."

Bill said, "She knew about your real name before I did?" Stacy answered, "Yep, that is how girls are and when I told her she damn near fell off her chair."

"Now that I think about it, Adam did have a little girl but I do not remember ever meeting her." Stacy said, "Because dad moved around so much I spent most of my life with my mom's parents." Bill said, "I think I like Dixie best." Stacy said "I think sailors like big titted, big assed redheads best." "If that is what it takes, I can get out my Dixie costume to get you all hot and bothered." With that, they lay back and had a great laugh.

"Wedding plans are put on hold until this operation is over; I have to go back in my Dixie role and Helen for a while longer. The board meets tomorrow and I will be there as Helen once more."

When the meeting was called to order the first to speak was Henry Green of the AFT. He said he had some good news that may surprise them. "The medical examiners are at a complete loss as to the cause of the illness and the deaths that are going around the country. There is not enough evidence to point to any reason for so many people getting this sick at one time. People are told that taking drugs can cause anything from lung problems to a heart attack. Here is the best thing about all of this, users are turning in the pushers to the police and are asking the government to protect them. They are so pissed off they are giving us names of dealers we did not even know about. We have put out the word that if you sell drugs to someone and they die you can be charged with murder. The smaller dealers are coming in to make a deal; so much that we need a lot of help to take care of the paperwork."

Admiral Collins told Henry that he would find some help for him somewhere. Naval intelligence said they are closing the noose around Caesar Markos' neck and are linking him to the warehouse in St. Louis under the Food for the Hungry banner.

Adams told the group, "There is one problem that the dealers may not be aware of and that is if the medical examiners cannot connect the drugs to these deaths then they are relatively safe from prosecution. He added, "Folks, we have them on the run; lets not let them up now." "Any other business? If not, meeting adjourned."

Adam came over to Bill and Helen and said how happy he was that they were going to be married and he hugged them both. It isn't everyday that a captain and a Lt. Commander get a hug from an admiral in the U.S. Navy. In fact it is never done, period!

Adam said, "I thought the medical people were smart enough to pick up on the reason people were getting sick. I guess Admiral Owings was right; this stuff disappears in the blood in hours."

Adam called the president on his private phone and told him the operation was going well. "Mister President, we have taken tons of narcotics off the streets, ships are bringing in a fraction of what they were three months ago. Any drugs found on a ship will restrict that ship from tying up to an American dock for five years. I know you will be hearing from the shipping industry on that one. We need help taking care of the paperwork because so many people are turning in the dealers that Henry Green and his staff are working around the clock"

"Adam," the president said, "I will look in to it today. Keep up the good work. You know that measures should have been taken a long time ago and maybe this drug problem may not have gotten out of control like it did. Ships that flew a friendly flag were overlooked and all the time they were dumping tons of narcotics on our shores. Now we will search every ship no matter what the shipping industry says. Not only that, we'll go over luggage and baggage on all planes. Hire the necessary people to do the job."

Adam said, "There is one thing you can do before you announce that you are not running for a second term. We have many great people that have worked such long hours and have not been home for weeks. They should be rewarded because without them we would still be back where we were years ago. I would like to see them kicked up one grade. Some are military and some civilian. There is one that I would like to see promoted from chief petty officer to a commissioned warrant. I know that is a big jump but this is the man that pulled my executive officer out of a burning plane suffering burns so bad that it requires him to retire. We both have seen some burning planes in our flying days, remember?"

"This all happened on that state department mission that I told you about, the one you were not supposed to know of. If it were not hush-hush, he would have been given a navy cross at least." The president said," you send me the list and I will take care of it." The next week Adam called the board meeting to order and announced that he was retiring and that this will be his last meeting. "I want to say that this is the finest group that I have ever had the privilege to serve with. After I hear all your reports I have some great news for you all"

The reports were pretty much the same as in the past: more ships and containers are being searched, borders are tighter, and the Caesar Markos organization has not only fallen, the underlings are making deals to save their skins and will testify against him.

"Thanks to your efforts, the streets of our country are much cleaner today. I hope you will give my replacement the same co-operation and loyalty you gave me. This board will continue in operation as long as politics stays the hell out of our way."

"The Alan Chime, the hazard burning ship that made its maiden voyage a few months ago, will be making regular stops around the country to pick up hazardous material including the narcotics from our collection station at Jacksonville Florida. We will continue to use the air station there as a collection point for the country," said Adam.

"Now, for the good news I promised you all. In recognition for exemplary work, that you did during our campaign there are rewards. Please hold your speeches and applauses till after the end of awards. As I call your name please step forward:

George Beck advanced to Assistant Director of US Customs

Roger Ralston, Advanced to full Commander, US Navy

Hal Ladan advances to Lt Commander, US Coast Guard

Brad Wilson advanced to Lt Colonel, US Marines.

Will Milford advanced to Lt. Colonel, US Army

Woody Miner advances to Major, California State Police

Mark Kent advances to Director, US border patrol

Henry green Advances to AFT Director, Mid-Atlantic region New Jersey to Key West Louis Newman of N.S.A. who kept track of ship movements coming to the U.S. has been advanced to director of hemisphere security.

Helen Able advances to full Commander, US Navy.

"Before I make any more announcements, I want you all to meet a real hero." Bill led a tall black chief petty officer down to the front of the room where Adam announced, "At great risk of his own life, this man went in to a burning plane and rescued Bill Story. In doing so, Toby Marshall burnt his hands so badly that months of plastic surgery brought him where he is today. He is being advanced to Chief Warrant Officer, U.S. Navy"

As Adam said this, Helen and Bill brought out a jacket and cap, and put it on Toby." Everybody applauded and tears ran from Toby's eyes. Adam said, "I know that everyone would like to shake his hand but that will not be possible for a few more months. He will retire on disability after that."

Adam said, "There is one more announcement; Bill Story will you come forward please?" Helen started to unbutton his coat and Bill wise cracked, "Please Helen, not here." Everybody knew that they were to be married shortly and gave a large applause. This was Helen's turn to be red faced. Adam came over and helped Helen to put a new coat on Bill. He did not have any notion of what was going on until he saw the wide stripes on his sleeve. They put a cap on Bill, and Adam said, "I want you all to meet the newest admiral in the US Navy," while gave him a big salute. Everyone went over to Toby and Bill and congratulated them on their big promotions.

Helen said to Toby, "Keep that uniform nice and pressed, there is a wedding coming up soon."

Bill retired - once a commander, once a captain and last but not least an admiral all in three-year period - probably a new record. Adam said, "There is one other promotion for a gentleman who is not here. That is the man that made our plan work. Bill Wilson, over at the shipyard, is now being promoted to Captain, USN."

Bill got busy lining up people to recommend Laura for entrance to the naval academy in Annapolis, Maryland. It was not all that hard, for Bill had many friends in spite of his being promoted over them. The fact that he retired did not change the promotion list one bit.

Helen's enlistment was up and Bill checked her separation papers DD 214 to see what name they put on them. She was listed as Stacy Collins and not by any of the many names she went by since he knew her. She moved in with Bill and started to make wedding plans. A small ceremony was planned at the chapel at the Naval Air Station over at North Island.

You never saw so much brass, from chief warrant officers up to full admirals. Adam gave his daughter way and the wedding party with Laura as maid of honor and Toby as best man. There were a million pictures taken. Toby drove the admiral's limo over the short distance to the El Coronado for the reception.

Helen said to Bill, "Even on this happiest day of my life, I worry about Dad." Bill said, "I have known your father for many years and could always know how to get in touch with him until lately. We will check in on him when we return from our honeymoon. I think he is getting treatment at one of the navy's medical centers."

The honeymoon started in London, then Paris, and on to Zermat, Switzerland. Here they traveled in cable cars to a high point in the Alps - over twelve thousand feet. The air was pure and you feel like you are top of the world, no dirt or odors until you get down at street level. Next they went to Rome and did some sight-seeing including Saint Peter's. Here in Rome, they saw the little cars they called 'Mickey Mouse' because the fenders looked like large ears. They would like to have been able to bring one back with them but - no chance.

Happy but tired, Helen and Bill stepped off the plane in New York with the intention of seeing some Broadway shows until Bill picked up a newspaper. The big headlines read 'Admiral Collins and President McClour are being investigated on unspecified charges.' Bill said, "Let's take the first flight we can to get home and see what this is all about. I know we tread on some toes during our workings but nothing to warrant a senate hearing."

The next day they went to see Adam to find out what all the headlines were about. Adam said, "We made a lot of people mad as hell when our men were promoted ahead of them so they got on the phone and called their senators to get them all in a huff. Some are even pissed-off because we cleaned up the streets which gives you an idea where their campaign money is coming from. No matter what, I will not let the president take the blame for anything. Just maybe they found out that he is not running for a second term. Don't worry I have some aces in the hole if things get too hot. They're also hot because we have one of their boys up on charges.

"In all the years I was in the navy, I could not open my mouth and now that I am retired, they cannot do much to me now. I have wanted to tell those feather merchants off for a long time. You see, they are all big shots but very low on guts. We are going to put people that give them money away for a long time."

"What can they do to me now - take away my pension that only runs until I die. They would like to shoot me but that would make them look bad. You know that I put everything I own in your names so they cannot touch that."

They ate that evening at the El Coronado. That evening; Adam looked up at the beautiful wood ceiling and said this place reminded him of an ark. "Getting back to money, one-half of my pension goes to The Saint Johns Orphanage here in San Diego. I used to go there every chance I got. A man I used to fly with many years ago before he entered the priesthood runs it. You may remember the name he used to go by. His name was Hap Owings - recognize the name? He is Dale Owings' younger brother and his name now is Father John. You never know how these hearings can turn out. They can make you sweat and say nasty things about your mother when they start to twist things around."

"I have been working on my sailboat to keep busy. It is great to sail around the harbor every chance I get, makes me realize how much I love the water."

The grand jury indicted Caesar Markos on drug charges and bail was set at one million dollars. It did not take long before high-priced lawyers from the largest law firms in the state were there to tell him he had nothing to worry about... He could afford the best and as his lawyers told him if everybody keeps their mouth shut, he will be home free.

Bill and Stacy were worrying about Adam, not only the senate hearing but because of the way he was handling his money. They thought there was more to the story than what he was telling them. Adam who was looking forward to the hearing said, "Let us take everything one step at a time."

After two weeks, Adam went to Washington and appeared before the seven senators up on an elevated platform. They like to look down on the accused as it gave them the feeling of power. The chairperson called the meeting to order. He said, "Mister Collins, you have read the charges; how do you plead?" Adam replied, "Sir, I do not plead. A person that pleads is asking for a lighter sentence. I am here to answer your questions to the best of my ability." "Mr. Collins, you are charged with violating the rights of people while you were in charge of the drug investigation," stated the senior senator.

"First off, Senator, it is you that should be here answering to charges that you let the people down by passing laws that restrict the workings of the law enforcement community. Also by giving drug dealers and criminals so much freedom within the laws that it becomes a joke. We lock them up and before the officer gets the paperwork done, they are back on the street selling dope all over again. Pass some laws that put the police on at least an equal base; you cut the border patrol's and the coast guard's budget to a point they do not have money to put gas in their trucks and planes. None of you has ever been in the service and yet you think you know what a service man needs and wants. I looked up your voting record and you are the enemy. I want the television cameras to take your picture as you tell me how you voted on the military budget."

"You sit there looking good so the people think you know what is going on around the country and all the while, you do not see the people that voted for you until the next election. You are not doing the job that the people elected you to do. The president gave me a job that was not taken seriously for years. You took the election funds, were elected, and then did not have the balls to do anything to change what was wrong."

Adam continued, "During the last six months we collected thirty-five tons - for the media that is tons, of narcotics. Our streets are a lot cleaner because of our work. Maybe the money that was spent on drugs will now be spent on food for the children and pay for fuel to heat their homes. The money that is spent on drugs in this country comes into the trillions of dollars; let me tell you that is a lot of zeros."

The senators just sat there for no one had ever talked to them that way before. Not knowing what to say, the senator said, "Meeting adjourned until nine am tomorrow."

The senators met in safer quarters to talk over the situation. One said, "We have a tiger by the tail and do not have a way to let it go. We feel like we are on trial and it is damned uncomfortable." "Okay," said the chairman, "We will find another way to attack Collins on some other charges tomorrow."

That night Cal Williams called from Gulfport, Mississippi, for he had somehow tracked Adam down. He said, "I saw you on television today and you were great. I loved every part of it and the press ate it up. You said what most of us would like to say, but never get a chance. The senators are an example of how bad our government has gotten. The main reason I called was to say that you delivered thirty-five tons of narcotics to my ship and it was taken out to sea and burned. I will swear to that if necessary. Call me for any reason you need me."

Adam thanked Cal and said, "That is music to my ears - stay in touch."

The next morning the reporters met Adam as he got out of his car and they asked, "What kind of bombshell are you going to drop today, Admiral?" They followed him into the chambers and Adam noticed there were twice as many cameras then yesterday.

The chair called the meeting to order and stated, "Mr. Collins, yesterday you were completely out of order. You had no right to talk to us that way." Adam responded, "Senator, you all forget that you work for us and not the other way around."

Senator Percy, one of the lesser members, started the questioning. "You said that your people collected thirty-five tons of narcotics. We have information that a large sum of it was back on the streets to be sold." Adam said, "Sirs, anybody can start a rumor; you people do it all the time like right now. Bring in the person who told you this one. I would like to question him or her. Can you produce this person?" The senator said, "It is not one person, but is what is going around." Adam replied, "Would you want me to start a rumor that you a running around on your wife?" The press loved it.

.

"I delivered the thirty-five tons to the ship to be burned as I said and I can prove it if necessary." Another senator asked, "Where did the ship go to burn these drugs?" Adam said, "They go out to the middle of the ocean to a location that is a secret for national security reasons. The furnace burns at twenty five hundred degrees so there is no chance of pollution."

Senator Nolan, who wanted to be on television asked, "Is it true that people have gotten sick and even died from drugs that have leaked from your collection?" "Adam asked the senator, "Do you have any proof of that, such as an autopsy to back up what you say? My people watch the streets and hospitals to keep track of what is going on. You senators have not the faintest notion what is going on out there on the streets of our nation. Get off your asses and find out what is going on. You are cheating the taxpayers of their money. Let me add if you had any proof of what you all area asking, I would be in court today instead of here listening to this mockery. Senators, you are wasting my time and that of the taxpayers - Good day."

Adam stood up to leave when someone in the balcony applauded and before long the whole chamber was applauding. The television cameras were taking it all in; they even followed him out to his car. He became a national hero that day.

When Adam got home, he told Bill and Stacy that he never felt better in his life after telling those feather merchants a thing or two. He also told them that he would see them when they get back from the retired officers convention in Los Vegas. "Have a great time, do not worry about me, I will be just fine."

Everywhere they went at the convention people told them how much they admired Adam at the senate hearings - the way he told them off.

After three days Bill and Stacy returned to San Diego. They tried to call Adam, but his phone went unanswered. They started to call around, but no one had seen him in for almost a week. He told them he was going to work on his boat so they called the marina to see if they knew where he was. The people that knew him there said, "He sailed out two days ago - maybe he put in at one of the other boatyards." They called everywhere but got no answers. They were starting to worry for a small boat like his is dangerous out there at night. They decided to go around to his house; maybe there was a clue as where he went. They let themselves in, looked around, and called out - no reply. Bill found an envelope on the kitchen table and as he opened it up and started to read it, Stacy entered the room. She saw the expression on his face and asked what was wrong. He handed her the letter and she read it aloud.

"Dear Children, "I have been under treatment at the naval hospital for the last two years because I have an inoperative brain tumor that has advanced to a point that I can hardly see. The pain has gotten to a stage that is unbearable. Drugs are not doing a thing to help anymore. I am sailing my little boat off into the sunset upon the waters that I have loved all my life. An old sailor should go this way. Please do not try to find me; I do not want to be found."

"Bill, I have loved you like a son I never had, and the day that you married Stacy was the happiest day of my life. My life is now complete for I know that the two of you were meant for each other. I know you will make Stacy a wonderful husband. Stacy was the light of my life, God bless you and my godchild Laura.

"Bill and Stacy had a long cry before continuing. The letter had a P.S.,"Burn this letter after you read it. Just between us you know that half of my pension goes to the Saint Johns' orphanage and if the government finds out I am gone the money will stop."

Caesar Markos was indicted and his trial was scheduled to start in two weeks. The press was having a ball about it. Here was a congressional representative that was up on smuggling charges and dealing narcotics nationwide. The prosecution was worried that the charge would not stick unless they got a witness in this case. It was hard for many seemed to lose their memory and in many cases their lives.

The prosecution was worried for San Diego has such a large Latino population that convicting one of their own is near impossible without witnesses. Bail was set at one million dollars but on appeal was reduced to five hundred thousand. Caesar's lawyers told him that as long as everybody kept their mouths shut he would have no trouble and to post bail for himself and for Pete Marcona.

Across town, Hittose Vicea got in touch with Henry Green and said, "I am in the San Diego General Hospital and I saw you on television telling the little children not to get on drugs for it would ruin their lives. I would like to see you. Come to see me and bring all the cameras and equipment you have in order to record a statement."

Henry got there with a whole crew and started with the doctor and a nurse. They both testified that they had been treating Hittose for sometime and that he was of sound mind and knew what he was about to say."

"I, Hittose Vicea, being of sound mine wish to make a statement. I have known Caesar Markos most of his life and when his parents died in a fire, I paid his expenses through college and law school. He worked defending people of our village for three years and did a great job. One day he came to me and asked if I would watch his back during a meeting he had down on the docks. It looked like he was going to get in to the drug business but I was not sure. Out of the respect that I had for his parents, I said I would watch his back."

Hittose Vicea continued, "I went to my desk, got out a gun, that I have a license to carry, and joined Markos in his car. We rode down to the dock area where we met two men. Caesar got out to meet them as I stayed back leaning on Markos' car. Soon they were shouting at each other and Caesar pulled out his gun that I didn't know he had with him. There were four shots fired, all from Markos' gun. He put two bullets in each of them. I didn't know it was going to be that type of meeting and if I had I would not have gone. He ran back to the car as threw his gun in the water and said, "Let's get the hell out of here fast!"

Vicea continued, "I found out later that one of the men that was shot was a big man in the dope business and the other was his brother-in-law that was running for congress from our district. Since the candidate for congress was dead, they needed a man to take his place. Caesar was well liked so his name was put on the ballot and he won. Off to Washington he went, with that I thought we were rid off a big problem. Boy was I wrong. Being a congressman gave him more power to dig deeper into the drug trade. The shooting, I will never forget, all the shots fired were from Markos' gun. The police found that the other men's guns were clean. Caesar threw his gun into the harbor and didn't give it a second thought. I had to get this off my chest before I die. I hope you have it all on tape and film."

Just then the priest came in and Hittose said he would like to have him hear his confession and receive Holy Communion.

Henry Green and his crew were packing up ready to leave when the priest came out and said that Hittose Vicea had just passed away. Henry thought to himself, "Boy, that was playing it close."

Toby called Bill and asked if he and Stacy would join him that evening to meet a special person for dinner. At seven the car pulled up out front and Toby helped a young lady out. Stacy met them at the door and as Bill came forward Toby said, "I would like you both to meet Marie Thornton." She was a striking young woman and Stacy asked like so many had asked before, "Are you related to Leana Thornton?" She replied, "Yes, she was my grandmother."

They ate a great meal at the officers' club over at North Island and after dining Bill and Toby left so the girls could talk.

Stacy asked if they were getting serious. Marie said that she was but not too sure about Toby. Stacy asked if Toby ever told her that he pulled Bill out of a burning plane when they were overseas together. Marie said she knew that was how he had gotten his hands burned some time ago.

Bill asked Toby if ever told Marie that his name was really Washington? Toby replied, "No, do you think I should?" Bill told him that only three people know about the switch – "You, me and Stacy. She knows because of working so close with me, best not to stir up the ashes. There are no papers on the change; Marshall and Washington are both dead and you have no fingerprints."

The men returned to the table and Stacy just happened to mention that this was the same table where Bill had proposed to her. That was the cue for Toby to take Marie's hand and ask her to be his bride. Marie replied she would be happy and honored to be his bride. After a toast and things started to settle down Toby said, "Bill, you were in real estate so maybe you could steer me to a nice house near the ocean." Bill and Stacy started to laugh, "We have just the place for you," Bill said, "As a matter of fact I have a place you have been to many times." Bill reached into his pocket and gave Toby a set of keys to Adam's house "Here, take Marie out there when the sun is up high and see what she says about it."

When the girls got their heads together Bill took Toby aside and said, "We have shared a lot of secrets and here is another. The reason the house is for sale completely furnished is that Adam is not coming back." Bill then told him all the details about the sail boat and the pension that was to go to the orphans.

Toby took Marie to see Adam's house overlooking the pacific and she fell in love with it. With Adam away so much the furniture was covered over a good bit of the time so it was just like new.

Bill went down to his mailbox in front of his house one morning when a car with government tags pulled up. Two men got out and approached Bill and one of them asked if he were Bill Story. Bill asked them to tell him what their business before he answered. They were showing Bill their I.D. as Stacy came out of the house. She turned to Bill and asked who the men were and what their business was. Bill answered, 'These are government men wanting to know how they could get in touch with Adam."

Stacy asked what the nature of their business with Adam. The men said they had run across some artifacts that shown up in town and in questioning one of the store owners Adam Collins name came up. "All we have so far is that a tall black man brought all of the items into the shop and he was paid in cash. Stacy replied, "We have not seen or heard from Adam for some time and have no idea where he could be reached."

The men gave Bill their cards, thanked him and left. They had not been gone more than a few minutes when Toby and Marie pulled up. Toby asked, "I saw the car with government tags pull away, nothing serious I hope?" Bill answered, "No, just some agents trying to trace some artifacts that showed up in town and them though maybe Adam could help them." Toby said, "All the items were disposed of sometime ago and we were very careful how we did it. I do not think Adam could be any help them"

The girls had so much to talk about now that the wedding time as getting close. Like a groom Toby was getting very nervous. Bill said, "With Stacy there to help Marie everything will work out fine."

Meanwhile, Henry Green met with the chief of police and showed him the pictures with sound recording of the confession. After the officer got over the shock of seeing this he called in an assistant and said, "Send two men over to the Belmont hotel to pick up Caesar Markos right away. Next send some men to the airport and bus station with his picture. With all we have on him now, we cannot let him slip away. He knows the language and could fit right in anywhere."

Two officers approached the front desk at the Belmont and after showing identification said they would like to see Caesar Markos. The desk clerk said, "You are in luck as he is just checking out. In fact, that is his luggage on the bellman's cart right over there." A man matching Markos' build approached the bellman. Markos had shaved his mustache off and cut his hair, but when he tipped the bellman, they knew it was Markos. The two officers came up to him and said, "Tip the man plenty for where you are going you will not need any money." They told him he was under arrest but Markos said that he was out on bail and was free to travel anywhere he liked in the city limits. The officers put cuffs on him and told the desk clerk that someone would be around to pick up Marko's bags.

Toby's wedding was a beautiful event at the officers' club with Bill and Stacy standing for them. There were some friends from the hospital and sailors that Toby had made friends with along the way. Marie had friends that she worked with and of course, they took a million photos. Marie, having her grandmother's looks and dressed in a beautiful wedding gown, looked like something off an expensive magazine cover. After a long honeymoon, they would be ready to move in to Adam's home overlooking the ocean.

The officers that picked Markos up were lucky for when they brought him in he had a new passport with his new look on it and a ticket for Panama City in his pocket. The officers at the airport and bus station had a picture of him when he was released on bail. These photos had him with long hair a bush mustache, there was a good chance of them missing him and they would have lost him forever. During the time before they clamped down on him he had sent millions to countries in South America where he could of lived like a king.

Markos objected to being locked up like an animal and at this point he did not know about Hittose Vicea's little show. He demanded to see his attorneys; he paid them millions and wanted great service from them. The chief of police called his attorneys and told them what they had on Markos. The attorneys could see millions of fees going out the window as they went back into the cell area to see Markos. They stood outside Markos' little cubicle and told him that they quit. "How dare you quit after all the money I have paid you?" protested Markos.

The lawyers told him, "You do not understand. They have a dying man's confession and there is nothing that will break it. We have our reputation to think of and if we lose a case, it looks bad on our part." With that, they walked out the door and one turned to the other and said," I hope that last check he gave us, cleared. "

The next day Caesar was charged with the murder of the two men on the dock that night.

That night Markos asked to see a priest from his old neighborhood. The guard said he would check with his supervisor as that type of request is rarely denied. The supervisor said it would be okay as long as the priest stays outside the cell and is watched over by a guard close at hand. Caesar gave the guard the phone number where the priest could be reached. The desk sergeant made the call and in half an hour, a priest showed up. One guard warned the priest he was Catholic and knew what it was all about so do not pull anything. They searched the priest to make sure he had nothing he could pass to the prisoner. Markos knelt down, with the priest on the outside of the cell and gave his confession. The priest said he would like to offer up Holy Communion. He reached in his pocket and brought out a plastic container with the wafers in it and a small bottle of wine

"Hold on," said the catholic guard, "how do I know that the stuff is not poison?" With that, the priest offered the guard the container of wafers and told him to pick one. The guard picked through the selection and picked one. "Fine," said the priest, "now hold it in your fingers while I pour some of this wine on it." After he did that, the priest took it and put it in his mouth. "Satisfied?" said the priest.

The guard watched as the priest gave Markos communion. When the priest was finished, he took the heavy cross that was hanging around his neck and got close to the cell and waved it in the sign of the cross. Just then he dropped the case of wafers and small bottle of wine. He reached down to pick them up when the catholic guard said, "I will pick it up for you, Father."

Markos kissed the cross the priest had hanging from his waist and then the priest backed off.

The priest asked the guard to hand him what had fallen on the floor. He proceeded to wipe everything off then handed them back to the guard and said, "Oh, never mind I have plenty back at the church. Please throw them away for me." He picked up his cross and waved it at everyone and walked out the door. Markos lay back on his bunk and went to sleep.

The press was going out of their minds for there was a forty-eight hour news black out until things settled down. The guards looked in on Caesar from time to time and since he was asleep did not pay him too much mind.

The guard brought Markos a breakfast of toast, coffee, and jelly that had been all checked out. This was the only time he could have food that did not come out of a can. The guard called the prisoner but got no response. After a few minutes, the guard went out and got the desk sergeant and they both came in and unlocked the cell. The sergeant reached down and touched Caesar's neck. It was as cold as ice. He turned to the guard and said, "Oh my God, he is dead - lock the door and do not let anyone near him. I am going to call the captain. Meanwhile, do not talk to anyone - not a word."

The captain came in and asked, "What the hell is so important that you had to call me this early, couldn't you tell me over the phone?" The desk sergeant asked him to follow him into the cellblock. The guard opened up the door and the desk sergeant said, "Touch his neck." The captain did and said louder than he should have. "Good God, this man is dead! What happened?" The guard and the sergeant said, "We followed the rules that were set forth on his information sheet. We tasted the food, water, and nothing else, not even a candy bar was given to him."

"Okay, cover him up to make it look like he is sleeping - not a word of this to anyone, period!"

The captain directed the sergeant to get everybody that worked around this man in the last twenty-four hours and have them in the meeting room in half an hour. "Move it!"

Everyone was there wondering what it was all about as they gathered in the meeting room. The captain told the group that one of the prisoners had gotten sick during the night. It was necessary to go over the prisoner's info sheet with each of them to make sure the instructions had been followed to the letter. They went down the list and everyone that had worked the cells other than area one left the room. Everything came out the way things were instructed. All were allowed to leave except the ones guarding Markos. "We don't want the word to get out that our prisoners are getting sick for some reason, so please keep all this under your hats, okay?"

This left the six men that were on duty after six last night. This left two desk sergeants, two corporals, and two guards. "Okay," said the captain, "Here is the info sheet on Markos. Let's see what we have. All food and drink brought for Markos is to be canned - soups and sodas. The soups are to be heated in pots that have been cleaned first, no exceptions. His coveralls must be brand new, his footwear inspected, no shoe strings. He was showered and given a cavity searched, and was to have no visitors. Is that the way it was?"

The guard who was a Methodist said, "That is the way it was - I really should not say this - except, for the priest."

"You mean a priest was here to meet the prisoner? That is not on the info sheet. "Who authorized that?

The corporal said, "He asked for the priest and the lieutenant said it was okay as long as long as he stayed outside the cell and had no contact with the prisoner." The catholic corporal that was on duty said, "Captain, I am Catholic and after searching the priest, watched as he heard confession. There was no contact even as he offered communion. Before he did that I saw he had a plastic container of wafers and a small bottle of wine and before I let him do anything I asked, 'How do I know that these are not poisoned?' With that he asked me to take out any one of the wafers, which I did, he said to put it between two fingers, which I did. Next he poured a little wine over the wafer and he put it in his mouth and swallowed it. He put some wine in a little plastic cup and drank that. That showed me that all of this stuff was okay. He put a little wine on a wafer and gave it to Markos. That was all there was to it. No, contact what so ever."

The captain said, "You broke the rules no matter how well you watched; he was slipped something."

The corporal said, "Captain, I kept an eye on the priest and the prisoner every second and there could have been no transfer of anything." The captain then said, "Then how did he get the poison that was analyzed this morning and proved to be a fatal dose of strychnine. That stuff works in seconds; the prisoner was probably dead before the priest left the building."

"What was the name of the priest and how did we get in touch with him?"

"The desk sergeant said, "The corporal gave me the number to call and ask for father John."

The captain said, "Do you remember the number?"

"No," said the sergeant, "but I wrote it down in the logbook.

The captain said, "Get it, now!"

While waiting for the sergeant to return the corporal said," I remember the prisoner saying the priest was from his boyhood church, Saint Leo's."

The sergeant returned with the number that he called last night. The captain got a phonebook and he said to the officers, "Guess what?" "There is no Saint Leo's church in the San Diego area. Trace that number."

It only took a second to get the location from the phone company.

"That's great; we get a fake priest from a church that doesn't exist with a phone number of a pay phone outside of a bar on south side of town. I do not imagine that anyone in that bar knows anything about any of this."

"Sergeant, send a few officers over there and ask around if they have any information on a priest hanging around the bar or the pay phone outside."

"Okay, let us get back to the priest and the prisoner. Was there any contact at all? Let us go back over every second the priest was there."

The corporal said, "He came in, said the prisoner wanted to say confession, and have communion. Both knelt down about three feet apart for confession - no contact. Next, the priest wanted to give Holy Communion. I searched him and saw him taste the wafer and the wine. Everything checked out fine. They both knelt down as the priest gave me the wafer that had wine on it to put on the prisoner's tongue. Markos remained kneeling and the priest stood up. As he did, he dropped the wafers and the wine bottle and he leaned down to pick them up. Since I was closer to them, I picked them up and offered them to the priest. He asked if I would dispose of them for him as he had plenty at the church. Captain, that is all there was."

The guard that was not Catholic said, "Not being Catholic I was fascinated to see how the ritual was performed. One part I do not understand was when Markos was still kneeling and as the priest stood up, the prisoner reached though the bars, took the cross that was hanging down below the priest's waist, and put it in his mouth for a second. At first, I thought that he was kissing it, but he put it in his mouth."

The corporal said, "I didn't see that." The guard replied, "You were busy picking up the items the priest had dropped."

"That's it!" said the captain. "There was a capsule on the back of the priest's cross."

The news leaked out like it always does and the press was on it like a pack of mad dogs

The rainy night that Markos' mother came across the border to give birth to him in an American hospital was the beginning and his dying in an American jail, on a clear warm night, was the very end.

GOD BLESS THIS GREETY MAN, AND MAY HE HAVE MERCY ON HIS SOUL!!!!

... THE VERY END